COW GIRL

A NOVEL

JUDITH AYRES BURKE

BurkeField

Registered - The Writers Guild of America-East

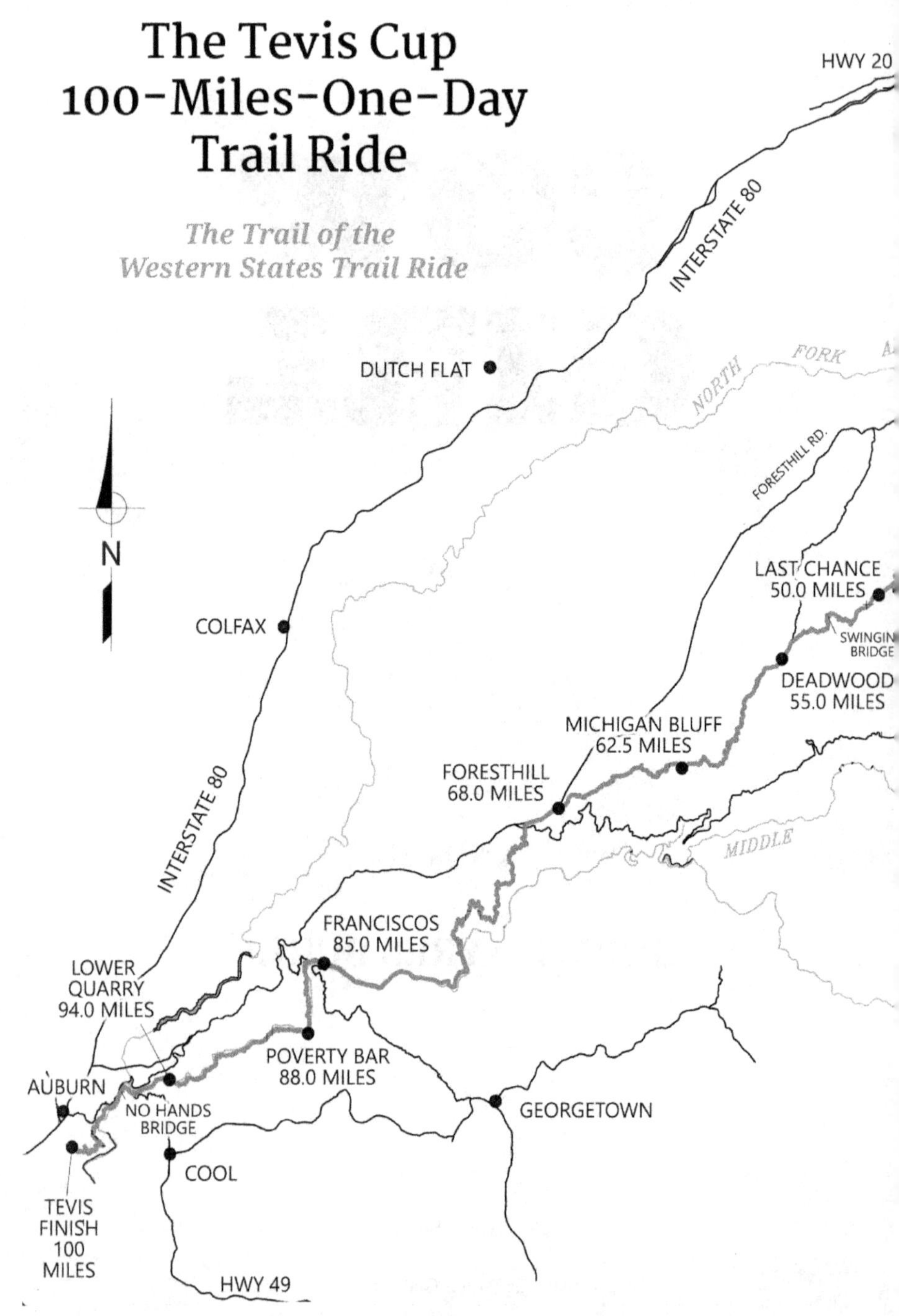

The Tevis Cup
100-Miles-One-Day
Trail Ride
The Trail of the
Western States Trail Ride
HWY 20
INTERSTATE 80
DUTCH FLAT
NORTH
FORK
FORESTHILL RD.
N
COLFAX
LAST CHANCE
50.0 MILES
SWINGIN
BRIDGE
DEADWOOD
55.0 MILES
MICHIGAN BLUFF
62.5 MILES
FORESTHILL
68.0 MILES
INTERSTATE 80
MIDDLE
FRANCISCOS
85.0 MILES
LOWER
QUARRY
94.0 MILES
POVERTY BAR
88.0 MILES
AUBURN
NO HANDS
BRIDGE
GEORGETOWN
COOL
TEVIS
FINISH
100
MILES
HWY 49

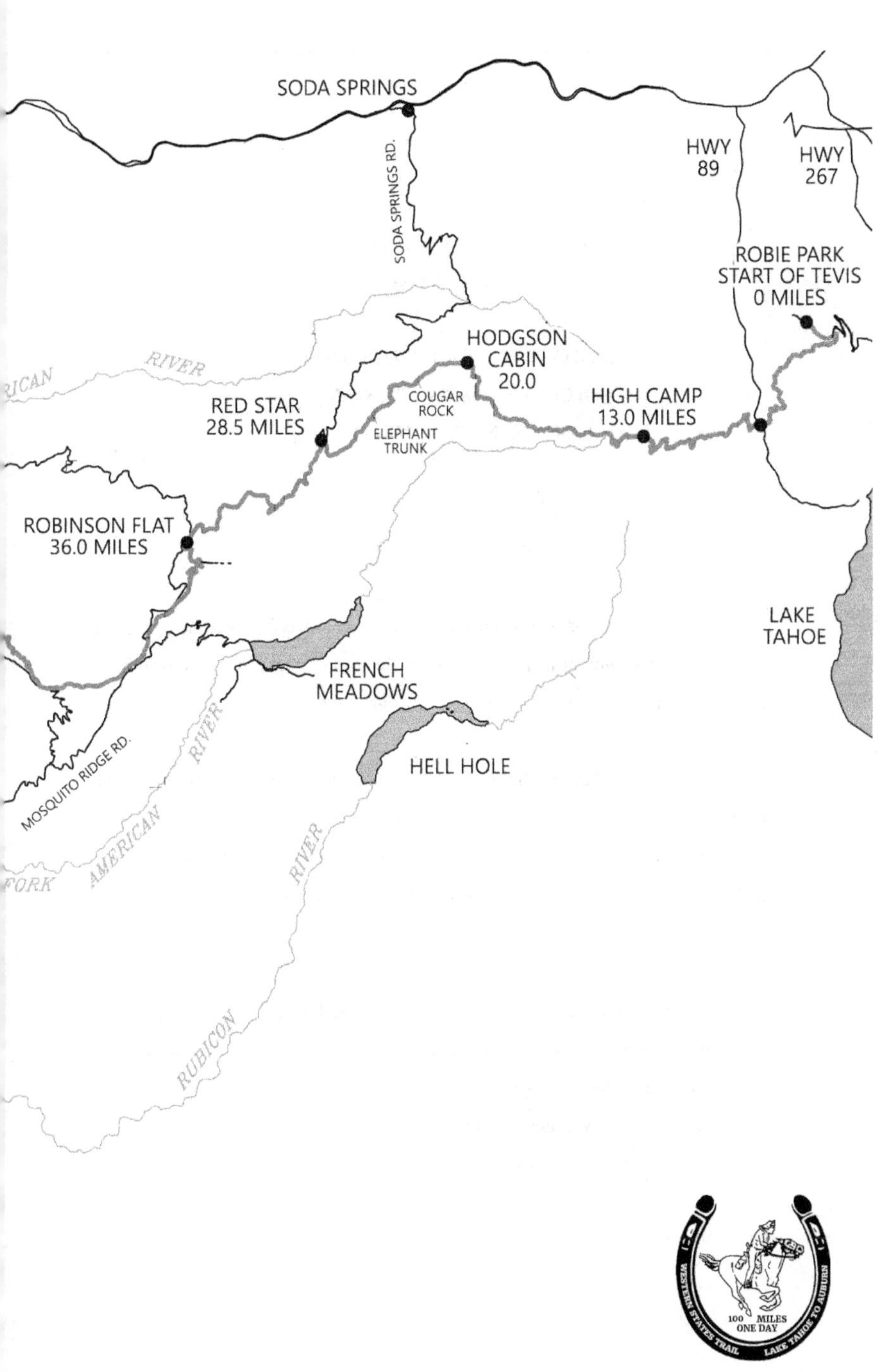
SODA SPRINGS
SODA SPRINGS RD.
HWY 89
HWY 267
ROBIE PARK
START OF TEVIS
0 MILES
HODGSON
CABIN
20.0
HIGH CAMP
13.0 MILES
RED STAR
28.5 MILES
COUGAR
ROCK
ELEPHANT
TRUNK
RICAN
RIVER
ROBINSON FLAT
36.0 MILES
LAKE
TAHOE
FRENCH
MEADOWS
HELL HOLE
MOSQUITO RIDGE RD.
RIVER
FORK
AMERICAN
RIVER
RUBICON
WESTERN STATES TRAIL
LAKE TAHOE TO AUBURN
100 MILES
ONE DAY

First published in the United States of America in 2019 by
BurkeField — Judith Ayres Burke
www.burkefield.com

Hard Cover: ISBN 978-1-7328137-0-0
Soft Cover: ISBN 978-1-7328137-1-7
Ebook: ISBN 978-1-7328137-2-4

This is a work of historical fiction. The Western States Trail Ride, known as the Tevis Cup, is an endurance horse race that occurs every year in the Sierra Nevada Mountain Range of California. The names, characters, businesses, places, events and incidents in this story are fictional. Any resemblance(s) to actual persons, living or dead, or actual events is purely coincidental.

Photography: Stephanie and Schuyler Knapp and Mark Nagel Photography
Tevis Buckle and Trail Map: With permission of the Western States Trail Foundation
Cover and Book Design: Judy Walker, judywalkerdesign.com
Website: Alex Dale, loudmark.com
Printer: Ingram Spark

Table of Contents

Authors Note	1
Chapter 1 ~ Start	3
Chapter 2 ~ Peak	16
Chapter 3 ~ Granite Chief	25
Chapter 4 ~ Elevation	31
Chapter 5 ~ Cougar Rock	37
Chapter 6 ~ Elephant Trunk	44
Chapter 7 ~ Red Star	50
Chapter 8 ~ Team	58
Chapter 9 ~ Robinson Flat	66
Chapter 10 ~ Bull Wreck	74
Chapter 11 ~ Hitch	85
Chapter 12 ~ The Point	93
Chapter 13 ~ Last Chance	102
Chapter 14 ~ Blood	111
Chapter 15 ~ Tempest	116
Chapter 16 ~ Hee-haw	125
Chapter 17 ~ El Dorado Canyon	133
Chapter 18 ~ Truth	141
Chapter 19 ~ Michigan Bluff	147
Chapter 20 ~ Onward	159
Chapter 21 ~ Darkness	164
Chapter 22 ~ The Work	170
Chapter 23 ~ American River	177
Chapter 24 ~ Window	186
Chapter 25 ~ Mule	194
Chapter 26 ~ "Go"	202
Chapter 27 ~ Black Hole of Calcutta	208
Chapter 28 ~ Finish Line	213
Epilogue	219

Acknowledgment

This author is filled with heartfelt gratitude for those many friends and family who have accompanied me on this literary endurance ride. Bountiful appreciation also goes to Jan Neuharth, friend and muse, who believed that this tale should be told. To Kinross Farm for graciously offering a quiet lair. To Hal Hall, John Crandell and others who generously shared moments of their dozens of Tevis rides and to Judy Walker, my book designer – a warm thank you goes to each. We have crossed the Sierra Nevada, together –

JEAB
BurkeField Farm
Middleburg, Virginia
2019

Dedication

To my family – Jack, Coventry, Davis, Spencer and Gilchrist – who have graciously endured this creative process and always believed in Cowgirl. Thank you.

My love - JEAB

BurkeField Farm
Middleburg, Virginia
2019

Author's Note

THE WESTERN STATES TRAIL RIDE, better known as the Tevis Cup—or, simply, the Tevis—is thought to be the oldest, most famous and difficult equestrian endurance ride in the world.

Tracing a path over the Sierra Nevada mountains first traveled by Gold Rush-era miners, the course covers one hundred miles of rugged, treacherous, and breathtakingly beautiful landscape.

The race draws approximately two hundred riders each year. Typically, fewer than half finish in the twenty-four hours allotted. Even as endurance horse racing has grown in popularity and other "One Day One Hundreds" have been established, the Tevis—held during the full moon nearest the first of August each year—is still considered the ultimate test of horse and horsemanship.

There are no monetary prizes associated with the ride. Competitors who finish in time win nothing more than a Tevis belt buckle. The horse found to be in the best condition among the top ten finishers wins the Haggin Cup. The first horse and rider to complete the course and be deemed "fit to continue" by a panel of veterinarians wins the most coveted prize in the sport: the Lloyd Tevis Cup.

Since the ride began in 1955, the Tevis Cup has been won most often by purebred Arabians. But it has also been won by part-bred Arabians, a Thoroughbred cross, an Anglo-Arab, even a mustang. It has been won by geldings, mares, and stallions; by white horses, bay horses, roans and chestnuts; by horses as young as six and as old as sixteen.

It has never been won by a mule of any sex, color or age.

Author's Note

Chapter

1

Start

THE HORSES KNEW there was trouble before anyone else.

You could tell from the way they were whinnying and nickering, shifting their weight and pawing the ground, snorting steam out their nostrils in the chilly predawn air; communicating their worries in horse language they know and the rest of us can only guess at.

When it comes to deducing the mysteries of science or solving complex equations, I'm not one to put too much stock in a horse's smarts. A typical Arab weighs around eight hundred pounds, and only twenty ounces of that is brain. But when it comes to sensing hazard, they are veritable geniuses...Einsteins with hooves. Horses have only been domesticated for five thousand years or so. For the fifty million years before that, their ancestors got on in this world by being the first to run away from bad stuff and the last to stop.

All it takes is for one to spook and the rest start acting up. And the more of them there are, the more distraught they become. Horses are herd animals, so you'd think they'd be fine around other horses. But a bunch of strange horses just adds to their stress. It turns out, like a lot of us, they're only comfortable with their own herd.

Imagine what it must have looked like at the start of the Tevis in 1985, when 199 horses—well, technically, 198 horses and one mule—all got skittish at the same time.

It was like a wave that came up from the back, going horse to horse, unsettling all of them until the starting line of the most famous endurance horse race in the world had turned into a big, jostling sea of equine angst.

Bit by bit, the riders began paying attention, too. Heads whipped back toward the cause of the commotion which seemed to be coming from an area near the lodge.

In 1985, the Tevis began at Squaw Valley, the ski resort made famous by the 1960 Winter Olympics. It was late July, so the lifts weren't in operation. But the folks who ran the resort turned the lift lights on to help illuminate the predawn.

In some ways that only added to the confusion, giving everyone shadows and casting faces in that not-quite-bright-enough light where you can't really see anything clearly.

Volunteers positioned to assist at the start were holding hand radios. When they began to squawk the same message, the humans finally caught on to what the horses had figured out a few minutes earlier: something was amiss.

"Medical emergency at the lodge. We need a doctor fast," the radios screeched, minutes before the 5 a.m. start. Which was a feverish enough time without throwing a medical emergency into the mix. Some of the riders craned their necks to scan the area near the lodge. It was too dark to really see much. Others immediately turned their attention back to their mounts, knowing that turmoil and horses are never a good mix.

Only one rider felt compelled to check out what was going on.

She was quite a sight, this woman. The kind of woman who, at thirty-eight, was still turning heads. She was beautiful, yes. But it was also because of the way she rode. The way she carried herself. She was five-foot-nine if she was an inch, a powerhouse of a woman with broad hips and shoulders, ample breasts and bulging thigh muscles. Her blond hair was plaited in a single thick braid that fell to her waist. Her tight Wranglers and red boots with pointy toes announced she was not one to trifle with. Take a package like that and give it the kind of serious sapphire-blue eyes that looked as if they were on loan from a marauding Viking, and folks take notice.

I think it only added to the mystery that she didn't talk much about herself. Folks knew she came from Lodi, a California ranching town. And they knew she showed up at the Tevis each year driving a pickup truck without hubcaps, hauling a faded red trailer that had "All-American Cowgirl 1977" emblazoned in foot-high, peeling white, block letters.

Which is why everyone called her Cowgirl.

The registration people probably knew her real name. It seems, few others did.

They had given her horse the number 188, which they painted on the horse's flank. Number 189 was assigned to Cowgirl's daughter, fourteen-year-old Lizzy, who was riding the Tevis for the first time. She was basically a coltish clone of her mother. She had the height, the corn silk hair in two braids instead of one and the blue eyes. Just not the hips and breasts. She wore a pair of sun-faded green leather chaps over riding pants and tennis shoes. Her left hand bore a splint that bound her index and middle fingers together. It was mending having been crushed between a halter rope and a tie rail when her mother's horse, unexpectedly, had pulled back and reared two months before. Just whose fault that might have been was an open question.

The registration people thought it was kind of charming, a mother and daughter riding the Tevis together.

Whatever was happening near the lodge was considerably less charming. As the radios continued with a burst of panicked talk, Cowgirl guided her horse over to one of the volunteers.

"What's going on back there?" she asked.

"Some guy's having a seizure."

"What guy?" she demanded.

"I dunno. Some poor guy in a wheelchair."

At the exact moment those words fell from the volunteer's mouth, the official starter, using a megaphone so his voice could be clearly heard throughout the lower bowl of the ski area, announced:

"Tevis riders, the trail is now open."

"Go!"

With that pronouncement, 197 horses surged up the mountain, taking the first steps of what their riders hoped would turn into a one hundred mile journey.

Cowgirl did not.

She tore off in the opposite direction. Back toward the lodge.

Toward the guy in the wheelchair.

Her husband.

You may think you've seen a lot of sorry sights in this world. It's unlikely you've seen anything quite as sorry as Cowgirl's husband.

Back in the day, when he was a rodeo heartthrob, he was a real looker. He had longish ash blond hair swept to the side and that certain crinkle by the eyes that women seem to be taken by. If that didn't do it for them, his tight Wranglers certainly did.

His body had been perfect for bull-riding: slim-hipped and wiry, taut muscle everywhere you looked. He coupled that with the flexibility of a willow switch, the balance of a dancer, and that certain gumption to hang on no matter what.

Over the years, working in eight-second gigs, he established himself as one of the best bull-riders in America.

As cowboys say, he was full of try. And he almost always succeeded.

There was a famous poster of him—right arm clamped to the bull rope, left arm pointing toward the sky, beaver hat at a jaunty angle—sitting firm atop a bull that was twisted so violently you'd swear it was trying to unscrew its front half from its back.

I have a copy of that poster at home. I look at it sometimes and think, man, that guy had everything: Looks. Youth. Money. Fame. Smarts. And, most of all, Cowgirl.

By 1985, eight years after the wreck, most of that was gone. The fame began to wane the moment he could no longer hop on a bull and thrill a crowd. The money went to medical bills. The looks disappeared behind the slack, expressionless mask that was now his face. There was no sign of the smarts, either. It was like whoever used to be at the controls had simply vacated. He mostly just stared off into space. If he could actually comprehend was another question.

After the doctors said there was nothing more they could do for her husband, Cowgirl brought him home to their little yellow bungalow in Lodi and set up a bed for him in the living room, where he could be in the middle of everything. She dressed him, spoon-fed him the baby food that his throat reflexively swallowed, and rubbed the cramps out of his legs when they had him yelping with pain in the middle of the night.

She did all that, day in and day out, because she loved him. And because, apparently, she had even more gumption than he did.

Cowgirl and her daughter always swore there was something going on in that cracked-up head of his. That they could see it in his eyes. I think it was more a prayer on Cowgirl's part, and, being a preacher's daughter, she prayed a lot. She was convinced he could understand everything going on around him. It's just that he was trapped in a body that wouldn't let him respond.

When visiting friends were being polite, they'd agree. They'd say he sparked up when Cowgirl entered the room or that he was looking lively because of some special occasion—Lizzy's birthday, Christmas, what have you.

But then, as soon as Lizzy and Cowgirl were out of earshot, the visitors would shake their heads and speak the truth. And the truth was pretty ugly.

Because, when you looked at the guy there was just nothing there. He couldn't even blink his eyes to let you know he understood what you were saying. You could go to the side of him and say his name, and you might as well have been talking to a water bucket. His arms—those arms that at one time refused to yield to even the toughest bucks and spins of a Brahman bull—now hung limp at his sides.

The doctors told Cowgirl he was in what they call a "persistent vegetative state." It meant he wasn't quite in a coma, because he actually did wake up and go to sleep. But he was a far piece from all the way there.

Sometimes, he cried for seemingly no reason at all. Or, perhaps, every reason in the world.

Because he was married to Cowgirl, everyone at the Tevis called him Cowboy. But that was just a courtesy. He was no kind of cowboy anymore.

As Cowgirl rode up to him, just outside Squaw Valley lodge, his eyes were rolled up and back so far you could barely see any of the deep green-blue iris of his eyes. His hips were straining against the seatbelt of the wheelchair, while the rest of his body flopped and trembled like a fish shocked to find itself at the bottom of a boat.

It's a cruel irony that a man who can't voluntarily move a muscle gets to wrenching around like that when his short-circuited brain goes off.

With Lizzy a few yards behind, Cowgirl jumped off her horse and rushed up to her husband.

No doctor had appeared. The guy who had taken charge was Hitch Jenson, also known as Doc Jenson. He was part of Cowgirl's support team, the Tevis equivalent of a pit crew. In previous years, Doc had actually headed the Tevis Vet Committee.

Doc was a large animal veterinarian who'd once been an EMT. Having Doc there was as good as it was going to get. Plus, Doc goes about six-foot-eight, 250 pounds.

"How long ago did it start?" Cowgirl asked.

"Been going for a little while now, " Doc replied.

Doc was holding down Cowboy's arms to prevent him from whacking himself in the face. Cowgirl knelt by his chair and put her hand on his twitching leg.

"It's okay, sweetheart," Cowgirl whispered. "I'm here, baby. I'm here."

"I'm here too, Daddy," Lizzy said, from the other side of his chair. "Love you, Daddy."

Cowboy kept jerking. He was in another world, that of a seizure.

"You're going to be okay, darling," Cowgirl said. "You're going to be okay. You're going—"

And then she stopped herself.

"Hitch, he's turning blue."

"Swallowed his tongue," Doc said, matter-of-factly.

When a medical professional says someone swallowed their tongue, they don't mean it literally. The tongue is a muscle, firmly rooted in the mouth. It can't be swallowed. But it can, during a seizure, slide backward and block the top of the windpipe, partially or fully, stopping airflow to the lungs.

"How long ago?"

"He'll be all right."

"How long?" Cowgirl demanded.

"I'm not sure. Haven't been here that long."

"Well, it's long enough he's turning blue. We've got to

go in there and get it out. Do you have anything in your bag that could force his jaw open?"

Doc kept his grip on Cowboy, but turned slightly toward her. "I do that and I'm going to break his jaw and a bunch of his teeth while I'm at it."

"His jaw isn't going to be much good to him if he's dead."

"Cowgirl," Doc said, as gently as he could, given that he was also holding down Cowboy as he thrashed but, ironically, did not struggle to inhale. "He doesn't have much time left as it is. And what time he has isn't going to be all that pleasant. Maybe this is...you know what the Tevis means to him. We're all right here with him. Maybe we should..."

"Don't you say it," Cowgirl brayed. "Don't you even think it."

Cowgirl fixed him with this look like she didn't care how big he was, she'd kick his ass all the way back to Lodi if she had to. Cowboy straightened for a moment, like a lightning bolt had traveled down his spine, then went back into spasm. His lips were paler now and his face was bluer.

"If you can't go in there and grab that tongue, I will," Cowgirl said.

She went for his jaw, trying to pry it open. But it was clenched tight.

"I'll do it," Doc said. "Choppy, I need my field bag."

Choppy was another member of the support team. His real name was Carlos Hernandez. He had dwarfism and was as small as Doc was huge, about forty-two inches tall.

"Pronto," he said, and hurried off to fetch the bag from Doc's pickup.

"What's your plan?" Cowgirl asked.

"I have bull-ring pliers in my field bag that might do it," he said.

Bull-ring pliers are used to install nose rings in livestock. But Doc was thinking they could also lever open a seizing man's jaw long enough that he could reach in and move Cowboy's tongue out of the way.

"Hang on, Dad," Lizzy said. "Help's coming."

"I'm not so certain he can hear you, Lizzy, but keep it up," Doc whispered.

"Daddy can hear me. He always hears me."

Cowboy bucked and strained some more. Choppy came running back.

"Here, Doc," he said.

"Switch places with me," Doc said to Cowgirl. "And hold him good. The quieter you can keep him, the less I'm going to have to hurt him."

The moment Doc stepped away, Cowgirl threw her arms around her husband holding him in the wheel chair. She was a strong woman. And there wasn't much muscle left on Cowboy. She had no problem subduing him.

Doc threw open his bag and tilted it upside down. All manner of equine equipment clattered to the ground. He bent down and came up with the pliers.

He moved toward Cowboy, flexing the end of the tool so its jaw opened, grimly ready to accomplish the same with Cowboy's.

Except a strange thing had happened to Cowboy. The moment Cowgirl put her arms around him, he began to relax. The thrashing and jerking slowed. His eyeballs rolled forward and the lids sunk as if they were too exhausted to stay fully open.

Any doctor will confirm—it's not possible to hug someone out of a seizure; not any more than it's possible for a person to will himself out of one simply because the right person is hugging him. But ask anyone who was there, and they'll tell you that's exactly what it looked like.

"Okay, he's coming around," Doc said. "Let's just give him a bit more time here."

"No," Cowgirl said. "He's not. He can't get enough air.

He needs air…do it now."

Doc frowned, like there wasn't a whole lot more damage left to be done to Cowboy. But he dropped the pliers and planted a waffle-maker-sized hand on Cowboy's chin. He yanked it open, stretching Cowboy's mouth wide, then went in with his index finger bent like a fishhook. Doc was a pro at going into horses' mouths. Cowboy's wasn't much different. Just smaller.

Seconds later, Doc announced, "There. Done."

Cowboy listed to the side of his wheelchair, having returned to his usual limp state. His face was a mess of mucus and tears, but at least his color was returning. Cowgirl gently kissed the top of his head.

"That's good, darling," she said, her soft voice having returned. "You just keep breathing now. Nice deep breaths. You're going to be okay. Lizzy, can you get a towel from the truck? We need to clean him up."

Lizzy bounded off alone. But, when she came back, she brought company.

Miss Betty was the third and final member of the support team, but also the unofficial boss of it. She was a retired emergency room nurse who had spent forty years being bled on and cried on more in a typical weekend than the rest of us are in a lifetime. Now closing in on seventy, she was tough as a walnut hull. Her weathered face squinted at Cowgirl.

"What are you still doing here, girl?" she demanded. "The race went off twenty minutes ago and it's that way."

She pointed up the mountain to the west, toward Emigrant Pass, to where a long line of Tevis race riders was already growing small in the distance. Their progress marked in the predawn by their headlamps, a string of bobbing jewels threaded on a far-away necklace.

"I'm not going," Cowgirl said. "We're done for today. We're not riding. Let's just pack up and head home."

"The hell you say," Betty volleyed back. "I got a truck

full of hay back there and if you don't give me some hungry animals to feed I'm going to have to eat it all myself. So get on with you."

"Miss Betty—"

"Don't you 'Miss Betty' me. You didn't do all that training and we didn't get all this ready so you could quit just because my friend here is having a bad morning. He's had his little fit, and now he's going to be fine."

"Look, if it happens again, I—"

"You hush now, girl. You know as well as I do he's never had more than one in a day. He ain't gonna start now. What do you think he'd tell you to do if he could talk?" Cowgirl surely knew the answer but she said nothing.

It was Lizzy who offered: "He'd tell you to cowboy up, Momma."

"Damn right he would," Betty said. "You just get along with you. I need to shovel him in the van and get us out to Robinson Flat. All you're doing is slowing me down with this nonsense. Now stop standing around everyone. There's work to do."

There were perhaps ten people on the planet who could prevail in a disagreement against Cowgirl. Miss Betty just happened to be one of them.

Without another word, she grabbed the handles of the wheelchair and started pushing Cowboy toward the parking lot.

"Well, you heard the woman," Doc said, already bending down and scooping his tools back into his bag. "Choppy, mind giving a hand with this?"

Choppy grinned, showing off the gold tooth that was one of his prize possessions. "*No problema*, Doc."

The small crowd that had gathered to stare at the seizure drama was slowly dispersing.

"Come on, Momma," Lizzy said. "You know this is what Dad wants."

Cowgirl surely knew that. But she stood, firmly rooted, a rare moment of indecision having come over her. Then she gave a little nod.

"Yep," she said. "The trail is now open for us."

"Go," Lizzy said.

Now, I should tell you, before we get too far into this, that while I personally witnessed that scene, there are a bunch of others I didn't see with my own eyes. The Tevis is a hundred mile race and you can't exactly watch it all from one set of bleachers.

I relied on a variety of folks to help me piece this tale together, making this the sum of a lot of people's recollections. Some came directly from Cowgirl—or, more likely, Lizzy, since she was always the bigger talker of the two. Some came from other riders who were on the trail with them, or the vets, or spectators, or some of the hundreds of volunteers who make the Tevis happen.

On race day, the Tevis becomes like one big family. And, luckily for me, it's a very chatty one. So I was able to hear about more or less their entire adventure, from start to finish and beyond.

There are parts you're going to think I'm making up or at least exaggerating.

But my earnest promise to you is that I'm not puffing this tale up in any way. The Tevis is big enough all by itself. All I really did was try to get things as accurately as I could, the way they actually happened. That's my promise to you.

Otherwise, I'm going to stay out of this as much as I can. This really isn't about me anyway. I didn't do a thing to help Cowgirl and Lizzy, nor do I have any official role or connection to the Tevis. I'm really just a hanger-on, a California, yarn-spinning, cowboy who will probably still be telling stories with his last breath. And this?

This is a story that needs to be told.

Chapter

2

Peak

THE FIRST FOUR-AND-A-HALF MILES of the Tevis is a straight shot up out of Squaw Valley. You're basically going up the mountain that rich folks in designer Gore-Tex spend all winter going down.

The Tevis doesn't use the actual ski slopes. The riders head up the service road off to one side. But the climb—all 2,550 vertical feet of it—is the same.

As Cowgirl and Lizzy got underway, they were already well behind the leaders, though I'm not sure how much that would have been on their minds. A handful of competitors come to the Western States Trail Ride each year with thoughts of winning the Tevis Cup. Everyone else is just hoping for a Tevis buckle—handcrafted from Comstock silver and gold and worth a lifetime of bragging rights.

This was Cowgirl's seventh try for a buckle. She had come away empty the first six times. She had always ridden by herself and completed the ride, in fine shape, just never in the time allowed. She had ridden mixed-breed horses that probably had as much a chance of finishing that race in twenty-four hours as I would hopping on one foot.

One of the Tevis veterans described Cowgirl as "a first-rate rider always aboard a third-rate horse." He may have been overestimating the horses.

Things were different this year, though no one was quite sure whether it was different good or different bad. This year, she was riding a white Arab mare named Piper.

Tevis folks had already gotten a good eyeball-full of Piper the year before. She was a magnificent-looking horse, maybe eight years old, a shade above fifteen hands, and one of the best natural runners anyone had ever seen—just supremely coordinated.

She was also a temperamental mess. Skittish. Neurotic. The classic million-dollar athlete with a ten-cent head.

Not quite knowing that, a man named Duke Dawson—one of those guys who fancied himself a contender for the Tevis Cup—had purchased her for $12,000, a big chunk of change for an Arab. Duke was always throwing his money around, but it still got everyone's attention. Especially when he arrived at the Tevis that previous year, 1984, and declared everyone else was vying for second.

Which is why some folks got extra enjoyment that he was one of the first to get bounced out. Piper was so nervous at the start, she was sweating from nose to tail. And she didn't get any better once the race was underway. The perspiration was falling off her in drops so big and fat that if you were underneath her, you'd swear you were in a cloudburst. By Robinson Flat, about a third of the way through, the veterinarian examining Piper had pulled her from the race because of severe dehydration.

Duke made a huge stink, of course. But it wasn't really a close call. When he realized he couldn't shout or bully his way out of it, he stormed around, cursing everything but the ground the animal trod.

"This horse is a worthless piece of shit!" he ranted. "I can't believe I paid twelve grand for this schizo!"

Cowgirl had ridden into the vet check on her third-rate horse just as Duke was winding up to offend some more. She said something like, "Nothing wrong with that horse, Duke."

Duke had been classmates with Cowgirl at Lodi High School way back. He had played Romeo to her Juliet in the school play. He'd been sweet on her ever since. Even if she never returned his affections, it was plain he was waiting around for busted-up Cowboy to finally be lost to the ages so he could be what Romeo might call her "bud of light." I'm quite sure he saw this as an opportunity to get a spark from Cowgirl's flint spirit.

Duke said, "You want her? You can have her."

It wasn't just talk. The next day, Duke had one of his barn hands deliver Piper to the ramshackle three-stall barn that sat just behind Cowgirl's tiny yellow house.

After a year of Cowgirl's training, no one knew quite what to expect from Piper. There was a lot of speculation—from Duke Dawson, but also from others who had seen Piper the previous year—that the horse was beyond rehabilitation, and Cowgirl was just setting herself up for another failure. But, for now, all reports from the race volunteers stationed along the trail were that the horse was looking good as Piper made that first, steep climb up toward Emigrant Pass.

It certainly helped that Jack was maybe two lengths behind her the whole time. Jack was Lizzy's mount, a gelded mule who was as loyal as he was smart. A mule is the offspring of a male donkey and a female horse.

Jack was huge for a mule, sixteen hands. He had ears like candlesticks and a massive head. He was a bay—three of his legs were black below the knee, and the rest of him was brown—and he had this way of half-closing his eyes, such that you'd swear he was actually dozing. Unlike most mules, who tend to be noisy creatures, Jack had never made a sound. Whether he was physically mute or just didn't have much to say, I'm not sure. No one had ever heard so much as a single braying hee-haw out of him.

He had been Lizzy's Christmas present when she turned

seven, right after the bull wreck that had put her dad in a wheelchair, when she needed a playmate more than ever. Jack was an incredibly patient and steady animal. He let Lizzy climb all over him, hug him, kiss his muzzle whatever she wanted to do. Lizzy wasn't near the horsewoman Cowgirl was and probably never would be. Her true passion was the violin. But she could handle almost anything as long as she was with Jack.

Which is not to say a mule got a lot of respect outside the family. The night before the race, when Lizzy first backed him out of that faded red trailer, there were folks laughing.

"What you gonna do with that thing," a ranch hand in a straw hat had shouted out, "hitch him up to a plow?"

Lizzy just smiled. But she wasn't smiling now, as the ponderosas and lodgepole pine trees grew shorter and the trail continued climbing toward the tree line. She had the serious, earnest look on her face she had been wearing ever since the lodge.

The grade was so steep the Arab and mule were basically just walking, so I imagine it would have made it easy for her to ask the question that had been working its way to the forefront of her teenaged mind.

"Mom, what was Doc going to say about Daddy before you cut him off?"

"Don't know what you're talking about," Cowgirl said.

Cowgirl had this non-verbal electric fence around her. Maybe, when she was younger, Lizzy would have known better than to try and touch it. But fourteen is an age for testing fences.

"Yes you do. Doc said something like Dad not having much time left and that 'maybe we should'—and then you cut him off. He was going to say maybe we should let him go, you know. That we were all there together…let him die."

Cowgirl rode in silence for a moment, pulling up the collar on the worn, fringed jacket she wore to protect herself from the cool, early morning mountain air.

What Doc had implied about Cowboy's clock winding down was true. Kidney failure was the culprit. One of his kidneys had been lacerated during the accident and had to be removed. The other had been bombarded with so much medication over the years—seizure drugs, antibiotics for all the infections he had suffered, analgesics for when Cowgirl insisted he was hurting—that it finally began shutting down.

There was nothing anyone could do about it. Cowboy was no kind of transplant candidate. Time on rural dialysis machines was precious enough that no doctor would give it to a man in Cowboy's advanced state of deterioration. To most of medical science, kidney failure or a final seizure would have looked like graceful mercy—or at least nature taking its course. Cowgirl was the only one who seemed to have other ideas.

"I suppose that's what he was going to say," Cowgirl said.

"Well...what do you...I mean, I'm not saying I want Dad to die, but—"

"Then what are you saying?" Cowgirl bristled.

"I don't know. I just...Momma, he's suffering. You have to see that."

"I see him having a seizure, yes. I'm not blind. But he's had them before and he'll have them again. It's part of his condition. You know that. There are 4.8 billion people in the world today. He's not the only one who has seizures."

"I know, but—"

"Well, then, that's just about enough."

And then Lizzy blurted out the thing she had been thinking for some time; the thing that she didn't dare say around the house, when her daddy was lying in his bed or sitting in his chair; when they were just trying to get through the delicate, difficult dance of care-giving duties that was their daily and nightly routine. It was something she probably only would have said out on an open trail, away from it all; and maybe only when it was still so dark she couldn't really see her mother's face.

"Have you ever thought about whether Daddy would even want to live like this?"

Cowgirl's posture stiffened in the saddle. Piper snorted softly as if she could sense Cowgirl's discomfort. Jack plodded a few steps behind, composed as ever.

"We'll talk about that some other time," Cowgirl said at last.

"When?"

"When the time is right."

"That's what you always say," Lizzy said.

"Well, then that's what I'm saying now."

A thundercloud came across Lizzy's face. She was by no means a sullen teenager. If anything, she went out of her way to be good most of the time, knowing just how full Cowgirl's corral was on a given day.

But I think she went into this adventure with the hope that her tight-lipped mother would finally start opening up a bit. And she wasn't ready for the disappointment that it would be business-as-usual on the one hundred miles of twisting trails.

"I'm tired of not talking," Lizzy spat. "I swear, sometimes the only person who talks less than Dad is you. I get so tired of it being quiet all the time. Do you know what it's like to go around hoping someone would just *say something*? I think half the reason I still pick up the violin is because at least the strings talk back to me."

"Keep your voice down, you'll spook Piper."

"I'm not. Keeping My Voice Down," Lizzy bleated, the sound bouncing off the granite ramparts and down into the valley below. "I know, I know, the time isn't right. But the time is never right. When is it ever going to be right?"

Cowgirl just worked her jaw muscles.

"I remember him, too, you know," Lizzy spat out, like it was a challenge.

"What's that supposed to mean?"

"I remember what he was like. You act like you're the only one who knows what he used to be, like I was just this little kid who didn't notice anything. But I remember how he used to lift me up and throw me around, how he'd pretend to be a bucking bronco and let me ride on his back, how he'd smother my face with kisses, how he braided my hair and read his cowboy poetry to me every night."

Cowgirl softened. "Well, good. I'm glad. Memories are precious, indeed. They're a precious part of life."

"Then why would you want him to go on like this?"

"Like what?"

"Like...this. This shell of himself. I mean, he was so alive. He was so strong."

"He's still alive," Cowgirl said. "And he's still strong. He's stronger than anyone you'll ever meet. Just not in ways most people can see."

The words had a certain effect on Lizzy, took the fight right out of her. Cowboy would have understood what Lizzy was saying. He would have surely forgiven her for it, but he wasn't exactly in a condition to speak up.

Cowgirl, eager to change the subject, said, "How's your hand doing?"

"It's fine, Mom," Lizzy said. "Just stop asking, please!"

"Okay. Now we're about to get some snow on the trail up ahead. You just let Jack handle it. He's plenty surefooted. Don't worry if he slips a little."

Lizzy rode on in silence for a moment.

"I remember him so well," she said to herself after a bit.

They continued their climb up from Squaw Valley without further conversation. This was about the time they were reaching one of those points on the Western States Trail that makes riding the Tevis one of the more stunning experiences a person can have.

It happens near the monument that marks the top of Emigrant Pass. You get this view that is at once soul-filling and visually luscious. The sun is finally starting to rise, just easing its way up over the horizon behind you to the east. Meanwhile, the full moon is setting in front of you to the west.

The ride is at its highest elevation at that point—8,774 feet, more than a mile and a half above sea level. The snow is still clinging stubbornly in the crevices of the giant boulders and amongst the shadows of the trees. Lake Tahoe, in all its azure realm, is spread out below. Squaw Peak is just off to your left. No wide-angle lens made can adequately capture the scene. It's simply too big.

There's something about looking down on that kind of perfection from that kind of height. Maybe it's because you're so high up you feel a little closer to your Maker. Or maybe it's because the air is so thin.

I just know that spot in the Tevis puts all kinds of profound thoughts in a person's head. Thoughts about hopes and dreams. Thoughts about life and death. Thoughts about whether we've added value to the world. Thoughts about why we're here and whether our life makes any difference at all.

And I can only speculate what Cowgirl was thinking as she reached that point. I would guess she was thinking about Cowboy and about why the Tevis had become her quest in the first place.

Cowboy had always been drawn to the Tevis—the history of it, the beauty of it, the challenge of it. He had ridden it once as a teenager and had quickly come to realize how ill-prepared he was for its extraordinary rigors. He had not won a buckle. The ride gave him even more respect for the Tevis, and he promised he would return and conquer it. The problem was the Tevis was held during the full moon nearest to the first of August, which was smack in the middle of rodeo season.

Back then, when he made the young man's mistake of thinking life was nothing but full of time, he always told Cowgirl that he was going to ride it again one day.

Correction: that they were going to ride it together.

"Someday, darling, we're going to retire from rodeo, and we're going to get us a couple of fast Arabs, and we're going to win the Tevis together," he'd say. "We'll finish one and two at the Tevis."

Cowgirl and Cowboy had been both sweethearts and classmates at Lodi High School. She had more than a bit of a competitive streak and had never quite gotten over the fact that he had finished as valedictorian, relegating her to salutatorian. Cowboy had also been the first Lodi High Merit Scholar finalist ever. He was gifted in many ways. So, she'd smile when Cowboy would mention their future family Tevis and say, "You mean two and one, my dear."

After Lizzy was born, Cowboy changed the end of his little dream to: "We'll be the first family to finish one, two, and three at the Tevis. And Lizzy will finish first. No question about it, Lizzy will finish first."

It was just silly banter, of course. And it was a dream that had disappeared, at least in its original form.

But dreams have a way of changing. That's what Cowgirl was always telling Lizzy.

And I have no doubt Cowgirl was thinking about it as the sun rose, the moon set, and she contemplated the last chance she'd have to win a Tevis buckle while her husband was still alive to see it.

Chapter

3

Granite Chief

THERE'S A SAYING AT THE TEVIS, shared among those who have run it many times and understand its supreme challenges: "You can't win the Tevis during the first third of the race. But you sure can lose it."

One of the first places that becomes abundantly clear is where Cowgirl and Lizzy were coming next. The Granite Chief Wilderness Area is a minefield of obstacles. There are huge boulders you have to steer around, shards of broken rock on the path, solid granite faces at odd angles. There's one section in particular, known as "the boulder bogs," where huge rocks are hidden underneath a foot or two of mushy muck. Any one of them can end your Tevis pronto.

Every horse at the Tevis—every horse currently in service to humanity—traces its ancestry to wild horses that used to run the steppes of Central Asia, a huge, grassy plain without a lot of hard surfaces. Arabian horses were then taken to the desert and bred to run long distances across sands and scrub.

As a result, most horses hate the feeling of solid rock under their hooves. It's just not natural to them. You can put titanium shoes on to give their hooves a better grip, but it only helps so much.

On such difficult footing, horses can slip and fall.

Or they'll come up lame after one of their hooves hits a rock at the wrong angle. Or they'll catch a sharp edge of a stone and cut their pastern or bruise the inner part of their hoof. Horses are very inventive about the ways they can injure themselves.

When that sort of thing happens, people will shake their heads, and tell the rider what bad luck it was. And that can certainly be true. But it's always struck me how the very best horsewomen and horsemen—the ones who really know what they're doing and keep their concentration on the task at hand—seem to have less ill fortune than everyone else.

Cowgirl was the best of horsewomen. Anyone who saw her riding Piper would have told you the connection between rider and horse was intuitive, that all Cowgirl had to do was think something and Piper would respond. In reality, Cowgirl's touch was so deft and her asks so light—a small squeeze of the legs, a subtle shift of the reins—that you could barely see them. And the instant Piper complied, Cowgirl eased off, giving that immediate feedback horses crave.

Jack and Lizzy were well synced, too. Their bond had been forged over the years, from knowing that each belonged to the other; that just as Jack was Lizzy's mule, Lizzy was Jack's human.

You would have thought, as the quartet reached the Granite Chief Wilderness Area, that they would have been as ready as anyone to tackle its rigorous terrain.

But Cowgirl had other thoughts. The Tevis course has changed many times through the years, and in 1985 riders were given a choice. To the right was the Sheepherder's Path, which was shorter and took riders through the jagged heart of Granite Chief. To the left was a gentler road that went down into the Little American Valley, the historic route that avoided the really tough stuff.

Cowgirl didn't hesitate when she reached the fork. She went left.

"Mom, what are you doing?" Lizzy asked from behind. "Sheepherder's Path is shorter."

"And more dangerous," Cowgirl said.

"But it'll take forever if we go the long way."

"Sheepherder's is too technical for us."

"You mean for me, Mom," Lizzy said, her voice getting louder.

"Besides, neither of the horses has splint boots. Our *team* isn't ready for something like that," Cowgirl calmly responded.

"I'll be fine. I can do it, Mom!"

"I know you think you can, but you've never ridden the boulder bogs. We don't have anything like that around Lodi."

"Well, I know. But I can do it. Jack can do it."

"We're going this way," Cowgirl said definitively heading toward the American River.

She was already a few hundred feet down the trail. Lizzy gave Jack a firm squeeze, urging the mule forward until he was even with Piper.

"Mom, come on," Lizzy said. "I know you want to protect me, but I'll be fine. Let's turn around and go the short way."

Cowgirl kept her sapphire eyes straight ahead, not saying a word. Lizzy legs squeezed Jack's side, urging him to a canter. Then she brought him to a sudden stop, turning him sideways, so she and the mule were blocking the narrow trail.

At that point, there was more than one dynamic at play. Among the humans, Cowgirl fancied herself in charge, and she probably still was—even if Lizzy was getting all kinds of ideas in her head about whether she wanted it to stay that way.

But equines have a pecking order, too. They establish it when they first meet, and it tends to be more rigid than the fluid dynamics of human interaction. Between these two animals it was quite clear Jack was the Alpha, though he chose to lead from behind on most occasions. Piper deferred to him.

With Jack blocking the path, Piper wasn't going anywhere.

"What the heck are you doing, girl?" Cowgirl asked.

"This is why you never win a buckle," Lizzy said. "We can save at least twenty minutes if we go on Sheepherder's. That could make all the difference at the end. We're already way far behind as it is. Do you want a buckle or not?"

Cowgirl sized up her daughter before speaking.

"You know when I was about your age I was Juliet in *Romeo and Juliet.*"

"What are you talking about?"

"I'm trying to tell you something here—"

"Well, then, yeah. I know. That creepy Duke Dawson talks about it all the time. He says he remembers all the lines but you don't remember any of them."

"So he thinks. But there's one line that definitely stuck with me. And it's one you best remember, too: 'Wisely, and slow. They stumble that run fast.' "

"And what does that mean? Can you please speak 1980's English?"

Cowgirl could have sat in her saddle and very patiently explained it to her daughter: that the Tevis is a long race, that she had spent six years watching the hotshots go out too fast and burn out their horses, that employing a little wisdom at the beginning would go a long way toward making sure everyone would make it through to the end.

But sometimes, especially with teenagers, less is more.

"You're just going to have to figure that out, dear one," she said.

Without another word, Cowgirl steered Piper through the small opening to the left of Jack and continued on her way.

Jack turned his huge head and watched them go. He stayed quiet, like always, but if he could have talked, you know he would have said, "Well, kid? What's it going to be?"

The Sheepherder's Trail was up on the ridge. Cowgirl's way was down toward the river valley.

It's been a minute since I was fourteen. And I certainly can't claim to have experienced it from the other side of the gender abyss. But there might not be a more confusing age for a girl. She wants to be a woman. She can't wait to be a woman. But part of her still wants to be a little girl, too, because she realizes how good she had it back then, when she didn't have all the expectations the world heaps on its women. Which is probably why your typical fourteen-year-old goes back and forth between the two so fast it can give you whiplash.

Consider Lizzy's green leather chaps, as just one example. She first got them around the time she got Jack, so she was maybe seven or eight. They were really little girl's chaps, except Choppy—who was quite the leather worker—kept adding strips to them, allowing her to keep wearing them long after she should have outgrown them. The original parts were now so sun-bleached, they were practically white. The strips Choppy added didn't match a bit. Lizzy kept wearing them all the same. She just couldn't let go.

You take a girl like that—now with scoops full of hormones swimming around in her blood—and then you toss a complicated mother-daughter relationship into the adolescent soup, with perhaps half a father thrown in, and you can see how things get tricky.

Some say, it is usually around age twelve that a girl reaches the shocking and often disillusioning conclusion that her mother really doesn't have all of life's answers. But maybe, at fourteen, she's finally getting the inkling that nobody else does, either.

I think that's what Lizzy was feeling, stuck in the middle

of that trail, not sure which way to go. And I can't say what, exactly, led her to make the choice she did.

But I do know when she finally made up her mind, she made a soft clicking noise with her tongue.

"Come on, Jack," she said.

Then she gently guided the mule in the direction of the valley.

Chapter

4

Elevation

AFTER THE LITTLE AMERICAN VALLEY TRAIL and Sheepherders' Path meet back up, the riders get to breathe a little sigh of relief and head down a logging road that cuts through the forest. It's wide and, compared to the ruggedness they've just come through for the first ten miles, quite gentle.

Still, some of the dangers of the Tevis aren't as obvious as a jagged boulder field or a big climb up a mountain. They're subtle, and they delve into things you can't see, unless you crawl into a horse's gut. Or hear, unless you have a stethoscope.

That's what Cowgirl and Lizzy were coming up against next.

Most of the riders who fail to finish the Tevis don't quit of their own accord. They get bounced out by a veterinarian, who is committed to being more concerned about the horse's health than about the belt buckle dreams of the rider.

With good reason. Horses will run themselves to death, if you let them.

It goes back to that fifty million years of evolution mentioned earlier. There was a long time when horses ran because they knew the tiger was going to eat the last member of the herd in line. Horses have never been very good at math. They run like they're last in line, even when they're not, even as their hat-box-sized hearts threaten to give out, because for a long time not running meant they were dead meat.

In these more or less tigerless times, horses need to be protected from that instinct. And sometimes Tevis riders, even though they care deeply for their animal partners, aren't always the best judges of when their equine friends have had too much. Which is why the folks who organize the Tevis established a series of vet checks.

The first of them was about fourteen miles in, a mile or two after the water stop at Hodgson's Cabin, up near a little crest on the trail known as Lyon Ridge.

Unlike the full vet checks later on, at Robinson Flat and Michigan Bluff, this was just a trot by. As the name suggests, the vet is supposed to watch the horse go by. Only horses that are obviously lame or visibly struggling get pulled.

For the leaders, this was no big deal. The best riders know how to pace their horses through the first part of the race, and the best horses are trained well enough that fourteen miles is little more than a light workout. They pass through Lyon Ridge with no trouble at all.

It shouldn't have been a big deal for Cowgirl or Lizzy either. Cowgirl had been training Piper for a year now, taking her on at least one long ride a week, and then two shorter ones as well. The horse was such a gifted runner, and the more she ran, the happier she was.

They often left at two or three in the morning and rode by starlight, both because so much of the Tevis happens during the darkness, which Cowgirl wanted the horse to be ready for and because that was the only time Cowgirl had to herself. The rest of the time she was working or caring for Cowboy.

Jack joined them on those rides, because it turned out Piper didn't like going much of anywhere without Jack. Lizzy rode on the weekends, when she didn't have school.

The rest of the time Cowgirl packed Jack down with two huge saddlebags, each filled with about sixty pounds of rounded river rocks wrapped in old saddle pads, so he would have the feeling of a rider's weight on him. The three of them covered thirty miles or more before most folks even woke for the day.

As a result, both horse and mule were incredibly fit. Fourteen miles, even at that high elevation, should not have stopped them from breezing through the first vet check.

Except, of course, the vet standing guard was Vernon Puce, an old codger in a leather bomber jacket who had more hair coming out his nose and ears than he did on his head.

Vernon wasn't an entirely bad sort. He had decades of experience and meant well enough. But he was born about the time that women got the right to vote and he still questioned the idea.

So even though Cowgirl and Lizzy came trotting up the hill in fine shape, both animals just as sound as could be, ol' Vernon walked out in the middle of the trail and stuck out his hands like a traffic cop.

"Whoa now, whoa," he said.

Cowgirl gave Piper a soft pull on the reins. The horse came to a reluctant stop, as if she didn't understand what the fuss was about. Jack and Lizzy came up even with them.

"Rider number one-eighty-eight and one-eight-nine," he said, looking down at a clipboard. "Heard about you two. A mother and a daughter riding the Tevis."

"Yep," is all Cowgirl said.

"You're the last ones to come through, you know. I've been waiting fifteen or twenty minutes for you. I was about to give up. I got other vet checks to get to. I thought maybe you had already packed it in."

"Just got a late start."

"Uh huh," the vet said. "Well, let's see how we're doing here."

He did a slow walk around Piper. "Good lookin' piece of horse flesh, this one. This was Duke Dawson's horse, am I right?"

"Yep," Cowgirl said.

"Uh huh," the vet said, though he had already moved on to examining Jack.

"Can't say that I've seen a mule coming through this year. Past years, yeah. Not this year. He's in last place among the horses but he's first place among the mules. Good for you, Mr. Long Ears."

"Yep," Lizzy said, mimicking her mother.

"What did you do to your hand, there?" he asked, nodding toward the obvious splint.

"Broke it," is all she said.

Puce ran a hand over his nearly bald head. "Well, that's a shame. How old are you, little lady?"

"Fourteen."

"Fourteen years old!" Vernon said, snorting out his hairy nose. "And look at you. Practically a woman already. Sure are easy on the eyes. I bet you're going to break a lot of hearts in a few years. Probably breaking them already, am I right?"

"Yes, sir," Lizzy said, because there wasn't really much of any good reply to a question like that.

"So tell me, L'il Miss Easy-on-the Eyes, what's your Daddy think about you being out here in all this rough-and-tumble stuff with a broken finger?"

Cowgirl stiffened, those Viking eyes staring a glacier full of ice at him.

Lizzy handled it: "He doesn't say much."

Ol' Vernon looked legitimately puzzled for a moment or two, then put it together. "Oh, that's right. Your Daddy is that fella who had that bull wreck. Sure was sorry to hear about that."

"Thank you," Lizzy said. Because, again, what else was there to say?

Vernon crinkled his hairy nose up, licked his lips, and sucked in a lung full of air.

"Sad thing, a girl like you, not having a father. You're going to have suitors left and right. Need a father around to make sure they show some respect. Boys'll take advantage of a girl if they think there isn't a Daddy with a shotgun around to make them mind their manners."

Cowgirl had been doing her best to grit her teeth and stay quiet so they could get on with the race. But this last pronouncement was too much for her.

"What does this have to do with the Arab and the mule?" she said, icily.

"Excuse me?"

"All this talk. What does any of it have to do with our mounts? You're here to check out the animals, not the riders."

There had probably not been a lot of women who spoke to Dr. Vernon Puce in this manner, and you can imagine just how much it pleased him.

"You telling me my business, woman?"

"I am when you're not getting to it. My husband and daughter are not your concern. The Arab and the mule are."

Puce glared at her from underneath a pair of wildly bushy, white eyebrows.

"Well, now that you mention it, the respiration on Mr. Long Ears here seems a little heavy."

Jack, having been stopped for a few minutes now, wasn't breathing any heavier than a newborn in its crib. Cowgirl had done enough endurance riding—where a horse's heart rate is considered such a critical number—that she could guess an animal's pulse just by looking at it. She normally wasn't off by more than a few beats. If she actually put her hand to the animal, she nailed it for sure.

So she reached out and touched the side of Jack's neck. She held her hand there for just a second or two.

"And yet his pulse couldn't be more than about forty-two right now," she said. "Isn't that something?"

They both knew a horse was generally considered fit to continue when its heart rate was able to quickly get down below sixty-four per minute.

Puce snorted again. "All right. You just carry on now. But I'm going to be keeping my eye on you two, y'hear?"

Lizzy didn't need to be told twice. She and Jack disappeared up over the ridge.

Cowgirl followed. But, first, she took an extra beat to stare a cartridge full of buckshot at Dr. Vernon Puce.

Chapter

5

Cougar Rock

IF YOU'VE EVER SEEN A PICTURE OF RIDERS doing the Tevis, chances are you've seen them atop their horse, leaning way forward, seemingly kissing their animal's ears as it scales a nearly vertical chunk of volcanic rock.

That's Cougar Rock. They call it that because there's one particular knob on the outcropping that looks like a cougar's head. It's probably the most famous single spot in the most famous endurance horserace in the world. And it's the obstacle Cowgirl and Lizzy were coming to next, a few miles further up the trail.

There are usually a few photographers stationed there, snapping pictures to sell to the riders later. What you'll notice in all those Cougar Rock pictures is that the rider is never looking at the camera, not even a little sideways glance or a pride-filled half-grin. They're staring straight ahead and down. Their entire focus is on climbing that rock, which towers several hundred feet and doesn't leave much margin for error. It's not quite a sheer cliff, but a tumble at the wrong spot would be like falling off the roof of a three-story house.

At the base of the rock were a small cluster of volunteers who were earnestly and vocally urging riders up. There was also a man off to the side, sitting on the ground, rubbing his legs.

His name was Woolfolk Henry. He was a lawyer for the Department of the Interior and a favorite of a lot of Tevis folks, because he had helped the organizers get permits to ride through the government land that covered the course.

Wooly, as everyone called him, went to Princeton. He was in his early forties and had never married. At six-foot-four, he was something of a gentle giant, with an easy smile and a graceful, gentlemanly way about him—an all around decent fellow. I'm not sure anyone had ever heard him say a cross word.

In two previous Tevis attempts, he had missed out on a buckle. He told folks that, whether he finished in time or not, doing the Tevis was the very best day of his year. That simply finishing was winning.

His horse, Laddy Boy, was a bay Thoroughbred who could have topped any of the Arabs in a sprint, but wasn't quite as formidable at marathon distances or when faced with the tricky footing in the Sierra Nevada, despite Wooly's attempts to train him up for it.

Wooly and Cowgirl knew each other casually, and if he sat up a little straighter when Cowgirl rode into view, it's because that's what men tended to do around Cowgirl.

The volunteers were already focusing their encouragements on Cowgirl and Lizzy, who would have been the last riders they needed to get up and over the rock. But Cowgirl steered Piper over toward Wooly.

"Hey, Wooly," she said, coming to a stop. "Everything okay?"

"Afraid not. I'm done for this year. We'll be heading back with some of the volunteers in a little bit."

"I don't understand. Laddy Boy couldn't make the climb?"

"The committee keeps talking about a bypass around Cougar Rock," he said, ignoring her question. "If they don't build it soon, I'm going to tell them the permits for Granite

Chief are too cumbersome to obtain."

He said this last part with a mischievous smile. Cowgirl had her head tilted. "But what's the matter? I'm sure Laddy Boy can handle it. He's done it in the past, hasn't he?"

"The horse is just fine. It's the rider who's the problem. I sit too tall to stay in the saddle for the steep parts without tipping Laddy Boy over. And I can't seem to make it up by myself this year. These things are just damn near worthless."

Wooly grimaced at his legs and went back to rubbing them. Lizzy, who had been quiet through the whole exchange, chirped up with, "What's the matter with your legs, sir?"

"Ever heard of a place called Vietnam?" Wooly asked.

"Yeah."

He left it at that.

I couldn't tell you who is the Patron Saint of Lost Causes. But at the Tevis, it was Cowgirl. I've heard that at least two of her failed attempts came because she spent too much time helping others get their buckles at the expense of her own. And she wasn't about to leave Wooly behind.

"Can Laddy Boy make it without you?"

"Sure he can, but what's that going to—"

"Well, then you can tail up with Jack here."

When a Tevis person talks about tailing up, they mean you literally grab a horse's tail and let it haul you up a steep slope.

"And your daughter rides Laddy Boy? Not a chance. My saddle is way too big for her. It wouldn't be safe."

"Jack can handle both of you."

"Oh, no. I'm sure that mule is plenty strong for Lizzy, but if you put the two of us together, it's a bit more than he bargained for," Wooly said, patting his stomach paunch. "I just worry we're going to get halfway up and he's going to tire out. Then all three of us will be stuck on that rock."

"Nonsense. And now you're just offending our mule. You better tell Jack you're sorry for doubting him."

Wooly took a moment to size up Jack, who stood there, eyes half-lidded, like he didn't have a care in the world.

"Now, come on, let's go," Cowgirl said. "We're wasting time."

The doubt in Wooly's eyes was quite plain. He flat-out didn't think the mule could do it. On a more gentle incline, sure. But not Cougar Rock.

"Now, Cowgirl, you're being very kind, but—"

"Wooly, you know I was a ranch calf roper? My best time was under ten seconds back then. I'm a little out of practice right now, but I swear I could still get you done in twelve. The problem is then you'd just be a big bundle of dead weight for Jack. It's better if you're on your feet. So come on, now, snap to soldier."

Wooly, with all his fine education, was smart enough to translate Cowgirl's decree. Still, he was shaking his head as he said, "Okay, then. Nothing beats failure like a try."

He stood up on his creaky, wounded legs and limped over toward the base of the rock. When the volunteers realized Wooly was going to give it another go, they got to cheering again. Cowgirl walked Piper over toward Laddy Boy, then took the thoroughbred's reins.

"We'll take the lead," she announced. "Jack's used to following Piper wherever she goes, so that's how we're going to do it here."

With Cowgirl urging them on, Piper and Laddy Boy began working their way up the rock.

"Okay, Jack," Wooly said, giving the mule a friendly pat on the rump as he grabbed the middle of his tail. "I hope you're as strong as advertised."

Lizzy quickly slid off her saddle and walked around so she could look into Jack's big, black eyes.

"You're okay, Jack. You got this, right? Let's get Mr. Wooly up to the top."

She gave Jack a kiss on the muzzle. Then she went

around behind him and tied a knot in the middle of Jack's tail for Wooly to hang onto. Once everyone was in position, she got back up in her saddle. The moment she touched her heels to Jack's side, the mule put his head down and started a slow walk up, the ripples of his muscles shining as they flexed in the early morning sun.

There are no official histories of the Tevis to consult on this particular subject. I am, however, reasonably certain no animal has ever hauled both a rider *and* a tailer up Cougar Rock. But I'll be damned if that isn't what Jack started to do.

The volunteers were whooping and hollering like wild, because they had never seen anything like it. Wooly was holding onto Jack's tail, letting himself be pulled along, almost like he was being mule-winched up the slope. And Jack, for his part, was all business.

There are two parts of Cougar Rock that give everyone the most difficulty, a pair of roughly ten-foot sections that shoot close to straight up. It's like asking a horse to climb a ladder made of hard rock.

Jack didn't seem to be having much trouble as he made his way up the first, one sure-footed step at a time. Wooly, meanwhile, was straining with each boot step. The big mule was doing most of the work, sure, but Wooly still had to make his damaged legs keep up their part of the bargain.

After that first section, there's a small ledge where the horses can catch a moment's rest if they want to. Except Jack hit that ledge and just kept powering up, like he didn't want to lose any of the momentum he had worked so hard to gain.

"That's it, Jack," Lizzy cheered. "You're doing it boy!"

And he was. Until he wasn't. Mid-way through the second big climb, he seemed to stall, coming to a dead stop perhaps five feet from the top.

This was the moment Wooly had feared and with good reason. There was no going down at that point. And up had suddenly become doubtful. Jack just seemed to have lost his steam.

"Come on, Jack," Wooly said, with urgency in his voice. "Don't stop now, ol' buddy."

Cowgirl, Piper and Laddy Boy were at the top by this point. And Cowgirl had turned them around to watch. They knew the trouble the second half of their party was suddenly in.

"Go, Jack," Cowgirl hollered. "You can do it! Dig deep! Climb on!"

But I don't think Jack was paying even the slightest bit of attention to Cowgirl. He was looking at Piper.

What was communicated between those two animals, I couldn't say. It may have been a little pep talk. Or maybe it was a challenge. Or maybe Jack just wanted to show off for his girl. But Lizzy later told me that as soon as Jack saw Piper standing perched at the top of that rock, with her Arab tail up in the air, it was like he got it in his mule head he needed to join her. And, as you know, once a mule gets his mind fixed on something, it's unlikely you'll talk him out of it.

The surge began from Jack's haunches as his back hooves ground into the rock and he gave it everything he had.

With one mighty forward charge, they were moving again. All three of them. Lizzy was leaning forward flat against Jack's neck. Wooly was just hanging on. His hands clenched even tighter above the knot in Jack's tail. Like that, they made that final piece of the climb, as Cowgirl hollered her throat raw.

When they got safely to the top, Lizzy hopped off and went around to give Jack another kiss or two. Wooly had collapsed in a heap. But when Cowgirl swung herself off Piper and went to help him up, he waved her off.

"I got it. I got it. Just give me a moment," he said, rubbing his legs and trying not to let the pain show on his face.

But he was smiling, too. "That's some mule you have there."

Jack, as usual, didn't make a sound. Piper was nickering.

Once Wooly got himself to his feet, he hobbled over to Laddy Boy's saddlebag and pulled out some apple chunks.

"I was saving this for later, but you earned it big fella," Wooly said, and began feeding the apples to Jack.

Soon, there was apple juice dripping out the front and sides of Jack's cavernous mouth. And then Piper walked over and tried to catch the juicy sweetness as it dripped out. It was a nice moment for the animals. For everyone.

It was Cowgirl who brought their focus back to the task at hand.

"All right, you big show off," she said, giving Jack a pat on the neck. "That's enough of that. We've got a lot of miles left to cover." The three riders saddled up, and soon they were off.

Chapter

6
Elephant Trunk

YOU'D THINK AFTER COUGAR ROCK, the gold miners who first hacked the Western States Trail out of the wilderness would have been eager for a break.

Maybe they just couldn't find one out there in the Sierra Nevada. Because shortly after Cougar Rock, Cowgirl and Lizzy, now with Wooly in their group, came upon a narrow ridge. It's known as Elephant Trunk, because that's how it's shaped—with a deep dip and then a curl up at the end.

It's not the shape of Elephant Trunk that makes it such a well-remembered, but not fondly, part of the ride. It's the height.

Interestingly enough, horses aren't the least bit troubled by a steep drop. There was never a time, out there on the endlessly flat Asian Steppes, when being afraid of heights would have given them a survival advantage. So they never developed it.

Humans have a different evolutionary story. We come from East Africa, where our ancestors had their choice of cliffs to fall off if they weren't careful. Therefore, many of us have a healthy fear of heights bred into us. Some more than others, yes. But no matter how tough you think you are, there are sections of the Tevis ride that terrify even the most stout-hearted rider. Elephant Trunk is one of those sections.

Cowgirl knew from experience that she just had to trust her horse, keep her eyes forward, and grit her way through it. To the horse, a flat trail at sea level is not so different from one that follows the razor edge top of a mountain ridge.

Lizzy didn't have that experience. And while she had heard stories about the Tevis, and about its many dizzying drop-offs, it was quite a different thing to see it from her Jack perch.

Especially when you're afraid of heights to begin with. Lizzy first learned about her fear as a little girl, when her Daddy wanted to hoist her high up on his shoulders, like daddies do. Lizzy was maybe three or four years old the first time she realized that was not her favorite thing. When she objected, Cowboy figured out what the matter was. It was piggyback rides from then on.

Ever since, she had avoided the edges of rooftops, high walkways made of grated metal, pretty much anything that would trigger that deep-seated terror in her.

But there was no avoiding Elephant Trunk, no safe way around. And Lizzy was a pretty good sport about things until she reached the first really gut-churning part. It's a spot where the trail has been carved into the side of the mountain, just a few feet of slick, crushed volcanic rock etched into the slope.

"Mom," Lizzy said, her voice already small.

"Yep," Cowgirl said.

"This is freaking me out."

"You'll be okay," Cowgirl said.

Lizzy's eyes cast to the left, down an incline that was nothing but jagged rock, canted at about a sixty degree angle, for a thousand feet or so until it disappeared into the trees.

As if to stoke her imagination, Jack's hoof knocked into a small piece of talus that slid off the edge of the trail and made an immediate drop down into the abyss. Lizzy watched it the whole way, pinging and bouncing and gaining speed, gravity doing what gravity does.

By the time it was all the way down, her stomach muscles were clenched tight.

"Mom," she said. "I don't think I can do this."

"You don't have to. Jack can."

Except, of course, Jack was part of the problem. There's something about being up in a saddle near a sheer drop that doubles down on your dread. Logically, the horse only adds maybe four feet to your total elevation. Falling from a mere thousand feet will kill you just as surely as falling from a thousand and four. But those extra four feet seem to have the effect of thrusting you closer to the sinking chasm, making it feel like you're at least another thousand feet in the air.

Without meaning to, Lizzy squeezed her legs against Jack's sides. She was just trying to hold on, of course. But Jack didn't know that. Confused, he jolted forward, banging his nose into Piper's rump.

Lizzy shrieked. Piper startled and sprang forward. Even Cowgirl sounded frightened.

"What the heck are you doing back there?" Cowgirl demanded.

"*I. Can't. Do This*," Lizzy said through clenched teeth. Her knuckles on her right hand were gripped so tight on the reins they had gone white. The fingers on her left hand that weren't immobilized by the splint had also curled into a ball.

From behind, Wooly suggested, "Close your eyes."

"I can't," Lizzy said.

"Well, then you have to relax," Cowgirl told her.

Telling someone to relax when they're on the verge of panic is not the most helpful guidance. But Cowgirl didn't have a lot of options. They were on the side of a mountain, hugging a single-track trail that was not much wider than a horse's girth. Cowgirl couldn't just hop off Piper and go back to check on Lizzy. Stopping wouldn't help, either. It would only prolong their dilemma.

Lizzy's breathing was getting dangerously quick. An adrenaline surge was making her shake.

"Mommy," she whined.

"Hush, girl, you're not helping anything."

The problem was that Lizzy couldn't take her eyes off that treacherous drop. Which was about to become an even a bigger problem.

Because they had finally reached the top of the ridge. It was a bevel edge, a rock suspension bridge just a very few feet wide. There was no more mountain on one side to provide at least a little bit of solid surface comfort. The drop was now on both sides, and it had grown to about two thousand feet. Whether Lizzy looked left or right, her only option was a deathly plunge.

For the girl who couldn't handle the prospect of a drop from her Daddy's shoulders, it was too much. She was now openly sobbing. Her heart was hammering in her chest. It was worse than her worst nightmare, because not even her bad dreams could dish out something like this. And there was no waking up to make it stop.

"I have to get off. I have to get off," she cried.

"Don't you dare," Cowgirl said, knowing that dismounting would have been the only thing more dangerous than riding. "You stay on Jack, you hear? He'll get you through this."

It's not like they could have turned around at that point. There was no way to go but forward. Which was a blessing, of course. Not that it felt that way for Lizzy.

As they continued across the ridge, the girl was finally beyond words. Her gasps and sobs were now more like moans. She had flattened herself against Jack's neck and was clinging to it so fiercely that poor Jack might have thought she was trying to strangle him.

Even Cowgirl was feeling it—not the fear of heights

but Lizzy's pain. There might not be a worse thing in the world, as a parent, than hearing your child suffer and not being able to do anything about it. Lizzy's audible misery was one thing. Her rapid respiration and the perilous effects of hyperventilation were the real dangers. Because she could just pass out.

And it's quite hard to hang on to a mule when you're unconscious.

They were in a bad spot. And there was nothing anyone could do about it.

Or, at least it seemed that way. And then Wooly, gentle Wooly, started to sing. The song he chose was "Somewhere Over the Rainbow," from the *Wizard of Oz*.

"When all the world is a hopeless jumble, and the raindrops tumble all around," he began. "Heaven...opens a magic lane."

It was soft at first, almost like an afterthought. But as the introduction continued, he grew louder. No one ever would have guessed it, but Wooly—government lawyer and veteran—also had a strong tenor voice.

"When all the clouds, darken up the skyway, there's a rainbow highway to be found. Leading...from your windowpane. To a place beyond the sun. Just a step beyond the rain."

As he reached the chorus—his broad, beautiful "Somewhere over the rainbow" soaring up the octave—something had quite clearly transformed Lizzy. Wooly's singing was washing over her like warm spring rain. The tension was easing out of her body. Her breathing was slowing.

And she had finally closed her eyes.

Cowgirl looked over her shoulder to take a peak because she couldn't believe what she was hearing and had to see it firsthand.

Wooly just winked at her and kept his song up all the

way across the ridge.

"Birds fly over the rainbow." And so, there in the high reaches of the Sierra Nevada, did three Tevis riders.

Chapter

7
Red Star

FOR PEOPLE FAR BACK IN THE PACK—and Cowgirl, Lizzy and Wooly were as far back as you could get—the next portion of the trail becomes mostly about eating dust.

Nearly two hundred horses can kick up a lot of the stuff, especially on that part of the ride. By that point in the summer, when rains are scarce and days are scorching, the footing is basically six inches of this fine powder that is beyond dry. It's red, iron-rich, and gritty, and it fills the air in a haze so thick you'd swear you were in San Francisco as the fog rolled in off the Pacific.

But, no, it's dust.

In a vain effort to fight it, Lizzy and Cowgirl both pulled bandanas out of their packs and tied them around their faces, leaving only their eyes exposed, bank-robber style. Last place Wooly was just squinting and blinking.

After a few miles, there was a hydration station, where some volunteers had hauled in enough water so all of the horses could get a drink.

Cowgirl knew she had to take advantage of every water stop she could. She pulled off the trail to let Piper and Jack fill up. Lizzy, still composing herself after the harrowing experience of Elephant Trunk, had wandered off to look at some of the wildflowers. That left Wooly and Cowgirl alone.

It was starting to get warm—or at least warmer than it had been at the start—so Cowgirl had shucked off her fringed jacket. Underneath, she wore a red, fitted snap-up shirt that went rather nicely with those snug Wranglers of hers.

"Thanks again for your help back at Cougar," Wooly said. "I couldn't have made it without you."

"Well, we wouldn't have made it without you at Elephant Trunk. Never knew you sang, Wooly."

"Oh, I'm full of surprises," he said.

Now, where Cowgirl was concerned, that would have been just about all the conversation she had in a typical day. Or week. Whether that was because she wasn't big on talking—or because she felt so fundamentally alone in this world—I couldn't say.

Wooly shifted his weight, shoved his hands in his pockets, and smiled in that easy way of his. "So how is your husband getting along these days?"

"He has his good days and his bad days. Not so different from the rest of us, I suppose."

"Well, yes, I suppose," Wooly said. Wooly would have known that Cowboy was dying. Wooly was a Tevis person. And Tevis people spend enough time around each other, especially in the days leading up to the race, that they get to chattering about everything under the sun.

And maybe some folks would have struck up a conversation with Cowgirl just to have something to feed the coconut pipeline. But I don't think that was Wooly's aim. I think he really cared.

"And how about you?" Wooly asked. "How are you getting along?"

"I'm getting," is all she replied.

"You've got a lot going on, for sure. It shouldn't be any of my concern, of course. But do you have anyone you talk to?"

Cowgirl thought about that for a moment, then came back with, "I talk to the Man in the Moon. He seldom talks back."

I'm not sure Cowgirl was trying to be funny, but Wooly laughed gently.

"Yeah, one good listener.

"Yep," she softly confirmed.

Piper, Jack and Laddy Boy still had their heads shoved deep in a nearby water trough.

Wooly cleared his throat of some of the dust that must have seemed permanently lodged there, then spoke again. "Forgive me, but the lawyer in me has to ask after your husband's accident, did you...were you able to get some compensation?"

"You mean, did we sue someone?"

"Well, yes."

"No. No one to sue. It was no one's fault."

That wasn't quite true, of course. There was someone they could have sued if they wanted to. And they probably would have won, too. But that wasn't Cowgirl's way.

"Well then, how do you get along?" He hesitated before saying more.

"I make pies," she said. "We sell them to the restaurants around Lodi."

"And is that...enough?"

"We get by."

What she didn't tell Wooly—or anyone, really—was that a hefty check came in each month from the Cowboy Up Foundation. It was something Miss Betty had arranged after the wreck, when Cowgirl's savings were gone and she was really starting to struggle. Cowboy didn't have insurance. His family was land rich but cash poor. And back then there was no kind of disability check for someone in Cowboy's line of work.

But the Cowboy Up Foundation allowed a disabled

cowboy, or his family, to apply for help. And, of course, Cowgirl's application had been approved. Without the largess from the Cowboy Up Foundation, Cowgirl would have really been in trouble.

Naturally, Cowgirl had still been too proud to even apply at first. But Miss Betty convinced her that's what the foundation had been set up for—people just like her and also that she'd be giving Cowboy a more comfortable life if they had a little extra. That was what did it. That and the lack of choice convinced her.

"Should your friends be concerned?" Wooly asked.

"I don't need anyone worrying about me."

"Everyone needs someone worrying about them."

Cowgirl sized him up for a moment, this kind, earnest, gentle lawyer from back east. Then she said, "I think the horses have topped off. Let's get a move on."

And move on they did. A few miles down the trail, they reached their next significant milestone, which was the Red Star Ridge gate-and-go.

There are multiple gate-and-goes spaced throughout the Tevis course. Before the ride begins, the competitors are given a veterinary card that they have to hand over as they enter the gate-and-go. The "gate" is more metaphorical than anything. Though the riders do pass through a gate of sorts to the vetting area. The card serves as its own governor, because riders can't continue unless a veterinarian has signed off at each stop.

The card contains information about all their previous stops, with various measurements of the horse's health and grades on its condition. The vet eyes it to make sure everything is up to snuff, looks over the horse, then checks the animal's pulse. The rider can't go again until the horse's pulse is down below sixty-four beats per minute.

For horses starting to struggle, this can be a ten or twenty minute wait. If it takes much longer than that, it's a sign of distress and the vet will politely inform the rider that, for them, the Tevis has come to an end.

Red Star Ridge is about twenty-eight miles from Squaw Valley, further than a human's marathon. Horses are much better runners than humans, of course. But twenty-eight miles is still twenty-eight miles.

By the time Cowgirl, Lizzy and Wooly pulled into Red Star, it was nearing 9:30 in the morning, more than four hours since the start.

The leaders, Duke Dawson among them, had come and gone, mostly without trouble. Others hadn't fared as well. Of the original 199 teams entered, eighteen were already out of the race.

As Cowgirl rode in, she passed one of the horses that had been disqualified. He was a gelding that was trying to urinate. Except no urine was coming out and the poor guy looked absolutely miserable.

This is what horse people call tying up. The official veterinary diagnosis is "exertional rhabdomyolysis." It's a mouthful of a term that breaks down pretty easily. Rhabdo comes from a Greek word that means "rod like" and myology is the study of muscles.

In other words, the horse's muscles have gone stiff like rods. The horse has essentially entered into a cramp that affects either part or, in extreme cases, all, of its body. When you feel its muscles, particularly its back straps, they're so hard you'd think you were petting a fence board.

Cowgirl glanced at the suffering animal, then turned her attention back to her own. She guided Piper over to a slender vet with her brunette hair pulled tightly back into a ponytail.

"Number one-eighty-eight and one-eighty-nine," the vet said, consulting her list as she accepted Cowgirl and Lizzy's vet cards.

"You can call them Piper and Jack," Lizzy volunteered.

"Oh yes. Doctor Puce radioed ahead about these horses. He said we should give them some extra scrutiny."

"That's funny," Cowgirl said. "He spent most of the trot by checking out my daughter and me."

The vet raised her eyebrows slightly, then smiled. "Well, I can't say I'm surprised. The first time he met me, he asked me what my husband did for a living. When I told him I didn't have a husband and wasn't interested in getting one, he looked like I should never have been allowed out of the kitchen."

The vet rolled her eyes. "Anyhow, these two are looking okay to me. Let me know when you think they've pulsed down."

Cowgirl briefly touched her hand to side of Piper's neck. "They're ready," she said.

The vet seemed circumspect despite herself. There weren't many horses that could travel twenty-eight miles up and down mountain ridges and get their heart rates below sixty-four beats per minute in the time that conversation had taken place.

"You sure?" the vet asked.

"Yep," Cowgirl said.

The vet shrugged, walked over to Piper, and brought her hand to the horse's jugular vein while looking at her watch.

"Well, how about that. Sixty," she said, then noted it on the card.

"And let's see about this guy." She walked over to Jack and repeated the procedure.

"Well, I'm impressed. I've got him at fifty-four," she said, giving Jack an affectionate pat. "I watched both these mounts trot in. They looked great. You are good to go as far as I'm concerned. There's hay and feed over there if you need it."

Cowgirl glanced over in the direction of Wooly, who

was still waiting for Laddy Boy to get his pulse down. He saw her look his way and waved her off. "We're going to be a little while," he said. "No need to wait for us. We'll catch up with you later. If all goes well, we'll see you in Auburn."

Auburn being where the race finished.

"Yep," Cowgirl said.

After giving Piper and Jack a chance to eat and drink, they pulled out.

The trail leading away from Red Star is a wide logging road. The footing is stony dirt that's been packed down by timber trucks. So the dust, while still considerable, isn't quite as bad as it has been.

It's a place during the Tevis where, if you feel like your horse is up to it, you can get a good canter going and really cover some ground. Unlike those first twenty-eight miles, which are almost all single track and limit you to the speed of the person ahead of you, you can start passing other riders if you feel your horse is up to it.

It's still high elevation, nearly seven thousand feet. But elevation doesn't bother horses like it does us. Because horses have huge spleens with a nearly inexhaustible supply of red blood cells for just such occasions.

Most importantly, it wasn't hot yet. Or at least not hot like it was going to get. The temperature was climbing, through the fifties and into sixties. But the air still had a crispness to it, and was filled with the pungent fragrance of the huge pine trees that towered on either side of the road.

Even cautious Cowgirl decided this was a moment when they could move it out a little and take advantage of the favorable conditions while they still had them. She and Lizzy actually did pass a few of their fellow competitors, giving them a friendly smile and nod.

The riders they passed reported back that Piper was almost flying along with the light, bouncy tempo of a butterfly. And big Jack was plowing forward like a locomotive with a schedule to keep.

The leaders were still a long way off. But for the first time, Piper and Jack—who so many Tevis folks had written off as a neurotic mess and a mule—were looking like a pair of mounts who just might deliver their riders a belt buckle after all.

Chapter

8
Team

A FEW MILES UP AHEAD, Cowgirl and Lizzy's support team was pulling into Robinson Flat, the first full vet check.

The Tevis attracts all kinds of riders. You have trim jocks, bald middle managers, precise teachers, talkative real estate brokers, public servants, intense scientists, ambitious cowpokes, fun-loving mechanics, well-fed philanthropists, starving artists, inspired poets, humble bluebloods, fit grandmothers—pretty much the gamut of horse society.

And yet, in its treatment of all these very different sorts of characters, the race really embodies the American ideal. The Tevis doesn't care who you are, where you came from, what your bank account says or how many degrees you hold. It metes out the same punishment for all comers, and the riders tend to be judged not on who they are, but on how well they take it.

The support teams are every bit as diverse as the riders they're helping out and are evaluated on the same practical, functional criteria. All that really matters is whether you can do the work.

So when I say that Tevis people looked at Cowgirl and Lizzy's pit crew as something of an oddity, it's not because they were being unkind. Most Tevis folks really do accept all kinds.

It's just that it was so peculiar, individually, and, even more so, collectively.

First you had Doc Jenson, all eighty inches of him. Then you had Choppy, all forty-two inches of him.

Then you had Cowboy with his blank eyes and his chin wet from the saliva, who had to be unloaded and wheeled around at every stop. If anyone suggested for a moment that he just stay in the van so he didn't get in anyone's way or be a bother to anyone or just because it would make life easier, Cowgirl would fix them with a kick-ass kind of look. To her, Cowboy was every bit as much a part of the team as anyone else. And she wouldn't stand for him being treated any differently.

Finally, there was Miss Betty. Cowgirl couldn't have told you how it was Miss Betty knew to stumble into the family. It happened not long after Cowboy's wreck. Cowgirl probably would have told you that sometimes fate just takes people who need each other and puts them together.

Cowgirl's need for Miss Betty was quite plain. Cowgirl couldn't afford home nursing care, yet there was no way she could have cared for Cowboy on her own, without help from another adult—not during those first difficult months or in any of the years that followed. Cowgirl also couldn't have spent all those long hours out on the trail, training for the Tevis, without Miss Betty around to mind the home front.

What Miss Betty needed from Cowgirl was a little more poignant. It turned out they were both grieving when they met, Cowgirl from the recent trauma and Miss Betty from a tragedy that happened long ago. Her husband and daughter had been riding in a car that was broadsided by a drunken tractor-trailer driver on Route 5. It killed them both instantly.

It probably killed Miss Betty, too, except she was still here. I think she had been looking for a new family ever since and had finally decided to adopt one. There's an old country saying that a woman needs to have a place to put her love. Cowgirl and Lizzy were the vessels for all the love Miss Betty could dish out.

Some of it was tough love, of course. That was the kind Miss Betty seemed to excel at. When she was taking care of Cowboy, she did so with the firm, decisive touch of a veteran nurse who didn't have the time or patience to shilly-shally around with anyone's feelings. If she felt Cowboy wasn't cooperating, she'd holler at him, even cuss him out sometimes, just like she had with any ornery, yet fully conscious patient.

I think that's why Cowgirl allowed Miss Betty into her home and into the inner reaches of her family so readily. It was the need, yes; but it was also that Miss Betty treated Cowboy the same way she treated everyone else.

She ruled the Tevis support team in a similar manner, with a no-nonsense approach; an iron fist in a rawhide glove.

So that was it, the team that was charged with getting Cowgirl, Piper, Lizzy and Jack over the mountains, down into the canyons and back again:

A giant. A dwarf. An invalid. And a tough old broad.

It was no wonder folks couldn't help but stare a little as that curious quartet arrived at Robinson Flat.

The first thing Miss Betty did was get Cowboy unloaded. She was driving the handicap accessible van that Cowgirl had purchased, already well-used, seven years earlier. It was now even more dusty and rusty than it had been back then, with enough miles on it to have traveled to the moon. As soon as Miss Betty came to a stop in the parking area down below the Robinson Flat campground, where all the horses would be entering, she went around to the side door. She opened it up and cranked the lift that lowered Cowboy to the ground.

Once she got him all the way down, she checked him out disapprovingly.

"Now, what are you still wearing that blanket for?" she

asked, as if it was his fault. "I know it was cold this morning but, land's sake, you're going to overheat if you keep that thing on."

She pulled the blanket off his lap. His legs were still clad in Wranglers, exactly the way they used to be. Except now, rather than hug his rock-hard thighs, the fabric sagged against his withered, useless legs.

The other thing you could now see were his boots. They were old and careworn, having been generally beat to hell. It was the same pair he used to wear before the accident. A few years ago, a well-meaning friend had given him a shiny new pair. Cowgirl left them in the closet. There was nothing that made it more obvious that a cowboy wasn't really a cowboy than shiny new, unscuffed boots.

Miss Betty wheeled Cowboy across the rough ground up toward the campground, letting him get bounced around a little because she firmly believed it was good for him. A body that doesn't get a little rough ground now and again can't stand any rough ground, she'd say. And that was no kind of way to live.

People stared at them as they went. Cowboy was still a kind of celebrity in that group, both for who he had been and for what he was now. Miss Betty didn't seem to notice. She was either used to it, or determined to ignore it.

Once she got him into the main tent and out of the sun, which was starting to get high and hot, she set the brake on his wheelchair. She looked down at him, trying not to notice the gray undertones of his skin that signaled just how advanced his kidney failure was becoming.

"You just stay here for a moment or two," she said, as if he had a choice. "I've got to help Mister Tall and Mister Taller get things ready for the horses."

Cowboy didn't respond. Because, of course, he always mutely stayed where he was parked.

"All right. Good man. I'll be back."

That left Cowboy alone. But not for long. As soon as Miss Betty was out of sight, a pair of ranch hands approached. One wore a straw hat. The other wore a baseball cap from a feed store. They were at the Tevis that day, simply as spectators.

"Hey there, Cowboy," Straw Hat said. "What's shakin'?" Feed Store laughed and said, "Nothing. And then everything. That's his problem."

Straw Hat snapped his fingers several times in front of Cowboy's face. "Can't believe this is the guy who won Grand Nationals three times. I mean, geez. There's nothing there. Check it out."

He snapped his fingers a few more times. Nothing on Cowboy moved. His eyes were as glassy as ever.

"Just a drooling mess," Feed Store said. "Sure married a hottie."

"Damn shame. That is much too fine a woman to be turned out to pasture."

Straw Hat was shaking his head. "Naw, I bet she's sharing time with that Mexican half-pint who's always running around after her."

Choppy was actually Costa Rican and "half-pint" has no place being applied to a fully-grown person, even if the height he grew to wasn't quite as full as some others. But these finer points of geography and language were lost on this pair of bullies.

Feed Store laughed. "That's right, Drooly. Now what you gonna do about it? Gonna fight him? "

"He's gonna drool on him, "Straw hat said.

Feed Store cracked up and took another pull from a beer can.

"Yep, that's right," he said. "You just drown that elf in drool, y' hear?"

They swaggered away, sharing a vicious laugh. Maybe a minute later, Cowboy blinked twice as his head slumped to the side.

A hundred yards of meadow away, in the area that had been assigned to entrants 188 and 189, Doc, Choppy and Miss Betty were hard at work.

The hay and feed had to be hauled up from the parking lot, where Doc had followed Miss Betty, driving a Ford F-350 with its bed fully loaded. They were also bringing up food for their riders, a canopy to shade them, sponges and water to cool off the equines. It was not exactly all the comforts of home, but it was close as they could get.

You might have thought that Doc, being the largest man on the team—the largest man in the whole campground for that matter—would have done most of the carrying. But, no, that was Choppy. He made up for the shortness of his legs with the speed at which he churned them.

If Miss Betty was there primarily because of Cowgirl, Choppy's allegiance was to Cowboy.

Choppy had grown up on the Guanacaste Plain, which is Costa Rican horse country. He developed a real good sense early on of how to care for them, and just had a nice, easy way around them. Choppy was a laid back, friendly sort who didn't let too much bother him. It was a disposition that made Choppy perfect for horses.

His nickname was an anglicized version of the Spanish word *chaparrito*. It translates to "short guy," but it's not derogatory. If anything, it's a term of endearment, and Choppy wore it with pride.

He had immigrated to the U.S. fifteen years earlier, selling everything he owned back in Central America to make the journey. He landed in Lodi because he had heard there was work there, and he got himself a job picking peaches, like a lot of migrants did.

Peaches have to be picked by hand, of course. And Choppy convinced the foreman that while he wasn't much good for reaching up into high places, he could climb in the trees and get to the peaches that men on ladders couldn't.

That worked out nicely for all involved, until the orchard owner came along one day and announced he didn't like some "troll" walking all over the branches of his trees.

Not long after, Cowboy came across Choppy, who was at that point a pretty sad sort: unemployed, broke, and stranded in a strange country. Cowboy's cash-poor father had taught his son at an early age that it made no sense to worry about what a man couldn't do as long as you found something he could do. And Cowboy, being class valedictorian, was smart enough to heed that advice.

It didn't take long for Cowboy to discover Choppy was an absolute whiz working with leather. At a ranch, like the one Cowboy's father ran, leather things were breaking all the time. So Cowboy convinced his father to hire Choppy anytime he needed something fixed, which was pretty much constantly.

Choppy never forgot that kindness and they became pals, a *Costa Rican immigrant* and a rancher's son. Each called the other "*hombre*," usually preceded by the word "my."

That maybe makes Cowboy sound like a purely magnanimous fellow, taking in the poor, picked-on migrant worker, but Cowboy was getting something from the deal, too. Cowboy was using Choppy's gift to his advantage on the rodeo circuit. Cowboy didn't touch a piece of leather tack that didn't have Choppy's hands on it first.

Once Lizzy came along, Choppy became a kind of playmate for her, too. Not fully realizing Choppy was a grown up, Lizzy allowed him full access into her world, with all its imagination, fun, and innocence. And Choppy had such a playful soul, with a soft spot for children, that he was all too happy to let the little girl think of him as a peer.

He even made leather dolls for her, stuffing them with horse hair. Lizzy's favorite was a tiny brown mule that she decided was a mare and, therefore, named Jenny. Lizzy carried Jenny almost everywhere. When Choppy came by to fix a saddle or perform some other task, he'd make up a new story for Lizzy about Jenny the Mule, who was always protecting her friends or off on some adventure. Lizzy grew to love Choppy's stories as much as she did the toy mule.

After the accident, a lot of Cowboy's friends drifted away. It was hard to blame them. Cowboy couldn't go hunting, fishing, or riding with them anymore, and he wasn't exactly much for conversation. It certainly didn't help that Cowgirl froze them out. Whether it was because she just didn't want them hanging around the house or because she didn't want them to see Cowboy in his diminished state, I couldn't say. She just made it as clear as she could—stopping just short of being terribly inhospitable about it—that they weren't welcome anymore.

But I don't think Cowgirl could have chased Choppy off with a switch. By that point, he was part of the family.

So it wasn't really a question of whether he would be a part of the Tevis team. It was simply assumed by all involved. And Tevis folks—well, most of them, anyway—never gave Choppy any bother about his size.

It went back to that American ideal, one that he very much was putting into practice in that meadow at Robinson Flat. Choppy could—and did—do the work.

Chapter

9

Robinson Flat

FOR ALL ITS JAGGED PEAKS and bottomless valleys and for all its deathly drop-offs and treacherous footing, no single place ends more Tevis dreams than a wide, grassy, basically featureless meadow one-third of the way into the race.

Robinson Flat isn't an obstacle because of anything that comes from nature. Its dangers are one hundred percent human-concocted.

In any given year, roughly a third of the riders that enter Robinson Flat as hopeful competitors leave as brokenhearted spectators. The standard Tevis organizers insist on is that a horse be deemed "fit to continue," by which they don't mean "fit to stagger on down the trail for a little longer." They want a horse that has another sixty-six miles or more in its tank, and they err on the side of the horse's health.

The things that can doom a horse at a vet check aren't always obvious to the naked eye. It's often what's going on inside the horse—with its metabolic processing and its hydration level—that results in its immediate disqualification.

So even though Piper and Jack seemed to be in fine form, Cowgirl knew that didn't necessarily mean anything. All it would take is Piper having too quiet a stomach or Jack not having drunk enough water for the ride to be over.

As a precaution, she slowed down to an easy trot for the last half-mile heading into the flat. She didn't want Piper and Jack coming in too hot. They slowed to a walk as they entered the clearing and looked for a vet.

Now, all the veterinarians are supposed to adhere to the same standards. And, for the most part, they do. Benchmarks are either met or not.

But not everything is a hundred percent black and white. There is some wiggle room, and vets who come back year after year get certain reputations. Longtime Tevis riders know the vets who are slightly more lenient, and others who are notoriously tough. The trick is, the riders don't get to pick and choose. They have to hand their cards to the first vet who becomes free.

To Cowgirl and Lizzy's relief, Vernon Puce was nowhere to be seen. But that relief was short-lived. Because what they got instead was an officious-looking guy with buzz-cut, salt-and-pepper hair. Everyone called him "Colonel," because he had been a veterinarian in the Army for twenty years. Whether he had achieved the rank of Colonel or not, I couldn't say. He surely acted like one.

"Number one-eighty-eight and one-eighty-nine," Cowgirl said. She was sitting a little straighter in her saddle. Her voice was higher than usual.

The Colonel nodded crisply as he accepted their vet cards. "Thank you. How's your ride going?"

"No troubles, sir."

"Well, I guess we'll see about that, won't we?" he said without a smile. "Let me know when you think their pulse is down."

"They're ready," Cowgirl said.

The Colonel's brow furrowed, but he offered no comment as he brought his hand to Piper's neck and consulted his watch for a few seconds. "Sixty-two," he said, a few moments later.

He wrote the number in his chart, then went to Jack.

Repeating the procedure, he finished by saying, "Fifty-six."

Then offered a taut, "Good," before noting it with the red pen he was using.

"You understand the new test we're doing this year?" he asked.

"Yep," said Cowgirl.

It was called Dr. Ridgeway's Test and all the competitors had heard about it during the pre-ride instructions. The horse had to trot out a precisely measured distance—thirty-nine yards—and then trot back again. Along the way, the vet watched the horse's gait for any signs of lameness.

But then, more importantly, the horse rested for a minute before having its pulse taken again. The number had to be the same or lower than it was when the test started. There was no chance to wait ten or twenty minutes.

Already that year, something like sixty horses had been flunked out at Robinson's Flat. More than half had failed Dr. Ridgeway's Test. The Colonel had personally disqualified at least a dozen himself.

"Okay, who's first?" he asked.

"I'll go," Lizzy volunteered.

Lizzy trotted big Jack out and back under the Colonel's watchful eye. Then, keeping his attention on his wristwatch the whole time, the Colonel waited precisely sixty seconds before taking Jack's pulse.

He looked down and noted the number in his chart as Cowgirl and Lizzy waited expectantly. When he looked back up, and saw mother and daughter staring at him, he said, "Fifty-six."

Lizzy didn't have time to relax. The Colonel had already sprung into action, poking and prodding various parts of Jack's body, performing the battery of tests that are part of the Tevis protocol: the capillary refill test (a pinch of the gums to see how quickly color returns); the skin tenting test (a pinch of the side of the neck to measure how soon it returns to flat);

the mucus membrane check (should be pinkish and moist); the anal retentive tone check (should be tight); and so on.

Most of them are designed to determine whether a horse's hydration is adequate. So, for example, if the skin takes more than five seconds after being pinched to return to flat, it's a sign the animal hasn't been taking enough water. And the vets know: if dehydration has set in already, before the really hot part of the day, there's very little chance the animal will ever be able to recover once the temperature soars. That's why so many riders fail to get their cards signed at Robinson Flat.

The Colonel worked quickly, with efficient and practiced movements. The last thing he did was bring his stethoscope to Jack's underside and listen for gut sounds, a sign that the mule was still digesting food and was therefore likely to have the energy needed to continue.

Lizzy was holding her breath through most of it. She had heard enough stories about the Tevis to know this was Jack's moment of truth.

Once he was through, the Colonel said just two words: "He's fine."

Lizzy huffed an audible sigh of relief. The Colonel made a few marks on her card, then returned it to her.

"Next," The Colonel said.

Cowgirl gave Piper a light squeeze and the mare sprang to life, briskly trotting out the thirty-nine yards of Dr. Ridgeway's Test, then returning with her head high, like she was fully aware she was being evaluated.

The Colonel's gaze went immediately from the horse's legs back down to his wristwatch, where the second hand was at seventeen. When it reached seventeen again, his hand touched Piper's neck.

Cowgirl was looking at him the whole time. When he was done, he returned his attention to her vet card. He was shaking his head slightly, but neither spoke, nor acknowledged Cowgirl's anxious gaze.

He went straight to the tests. It's often a combination of factors—more than any single result—that leads to a horse being declared unfit. So, for example, if a capillary refill test takes a little longer than a second, and then the skin tenting takes six seconds, and the anal retentive tone seems just slightly slack, none of those things individually would get a horse bounced. But when you put them together, the vet gets a picture of a horse in beginning stages of distress.

It was unclear if that's what was happening with Piper. The Colonel wasn't saying a word. He was again finishing with the colic check, working his stethoscope over several parts of Piper's stomach. This was probably the part that worried Cowgirl the most, since Piper had refused to eat back at Red Star Ridge.

When he was through, The Colonel looked up at Cowgirl with a grim expression.

"This horse," he said, then added a pause, like he was trying to think of how best to formulate the news he needed to deliver.

Finally, he came up with: "Is in outstanding shape. Best I've seen today. Whatever you're doing with her, keep it up. You keep going like this, you're going to be in the running for the Haggin."

"Thank you, sir," Cowgirl said. She flashed a quick smile at Lizzy, who was beaming, even though she wasn't quite sure why.

"Good luck to you both," the Colonel said.

He was looking at them like he was thinking about saluting. Instead, he just handed Cowgirl her signed vet card and continued to his next rider in need of inspection.

"What's the Haggin?" Lizzy whispered as they led their animals away from the vet area.

"The Haggin Cup," Cowgirl said, "is given to the animal judged to have finished the race in the best shape. Some folks say it's every bit as prestigious as winning the Tevis."

"Wow, you think Piper could really do that?"

"I think," Cowgirl said, "we still have a long way to go."

After the relative solitude of the trail, the view that greeted Cowgirl and Lizzy as they entered the main staging ground at Robinson Flat would have seemed like chaos.

Unlike the earlier gate-and-go at Red Star Ridge, Robinson Flat is a gate and hold. After passing their vet check, the horses have a mandatory one-hour wait.

It makes the flat a bottleneck of sorts. The leaders are heading out just as the middle- and back-of-the-pack horses are heading in, but a good chunk of the competitors will find themselves there at roughly the same time.

That meant there were horses, volunteers, crew members and veterinarians everywhere, all of them with somewhere to be, all of them with something to do, and all of them in a hurry to do it. Even though the Tevis stretches twenty-four hours, no one forgets for a moment it's a race. It's a tornado of activity.

So after Piper and Jack passed their big test, Cowgirl and Lizzy flunked theirs: they couldn't find their support team. They rode in a big semicircle around the flat, searching in vain.

When they reached the far end of the clearing, they finally saw a familiar face. It just wasn't the one they were looking for.

Duke Dawson was just about to resume his race, having passed through the vet check and the one-hour hold. He was sitting tall on his new horse, a frisky seven-year-old Arab stallion he called Diesel.

The name was a nod to Duke's line of work. Duke's father had owned a filling station in Lodi, and Duke had worked there as a boy, pumping fuel and selling sodas to people passing through. Over the ensuing years—with a few bank loans, some timely business decisions, and a sharp sense of what the American driving public desired—Duke had parlayed his father's one location into a chain of gas station/convenience stores throughout Northern California.

He now had more money than he knew what to do with. On top of that, he was a fine-looking fellow, tall and broad-shouldered, a former high school football star who hadn't allowed himself to grow soft like most of the rest of the team.

Between that and his money, there was a steady supply of women vying to be the first Mrs. Dawson. They all had big breasts, bigger hair and flawless manicures. The other thing they had in common was that none of them had been successful in their mission. Duke changed women faster than he did horses.

It was certainly possible Duke just enjoyed the bachelor life. There was also talk that Duke's heart had never moved on from Cowgirl. Her affection was the one thing in this world he ever truly wanted and had been unable to have. Sometimes I wondered: Did he really love her? Or was it just about winning? I couldn't say for sure. But I do know Duke Dawson loved to win—at everything.

When he saw Cowgirl, he spurred his stallion toward her. And, yes, Duke wore a set of big, shiny, jangly Clover Bar spurs. He was the only Tevis rider who did.

"Why, how now, Juliet," he said.

He was always calling her that.

"Hey, Duke," Cowgirl said. "You seen my crew by any chance?"

"Yeah, they're over there," he said, pointing toward the opposite edge of the clearing, the one she and Lizzy hadn't ridden near.

"Got it, thanks."

"Your ride going good?"

"Yep."

"I'm worried about that mare," he said. "Once a worthless piece, always one, I say."

"She's a fine horse, Duke."

"She sure as hell wasn't for me. I probably should have known better than to think I could reason with a female."

He laughed at his own joke.

"I have to say I'm real happy with Diesel, here," Duke said, not that anyone asked. "Been training him up since he was a colt, you know."

"Yep."

"People kept telling me I ought to cut him, but I just couldn't bring myself to. I think it gives 'em a special spirit, being left intact."

Cowgirl didn't reply. A lot of horse folks would have told you that stallions have a special spirit right up until the moment they quit on you. Then it's not so special.

"After he wins the Tevis for me, I'm thinking I'm going to breed him," Duke said. "Maybe Piper there can be his broodmare. He'd be great cover for her."

I'm sure that's not the only cover Duke Dawson had in mind.

Cowgirl just said, "See ya."

She turned and started riding in the direction Duke had pointed. Duke was forever trying to start conversations with Cowgirl and forever mystified as to why she didn't take him up on it.

"All right," he said to her half-turned back. "Well, guess I got a race to go and win now. I'll see you in Auburn. We should celebrate with a drink. Maybe two."

He watched her go, his eyes lingering over all that he wanted but didn't yet have.

Chapter

10
Bull Wreck

DOC AND CHOPPY HAD BEEN RESTING in the shade of their canopy, leaning against some hay bales. Miss Betty had been puttering around, taking out some treats for "her girls," as she called them, and making sure everything was just so.

They were on what might be called low alert. But that changed the moment Cowgirl and Lizzy came into view. Doc and Choppy leapt up. Miss Betty went into double time.

The reunion between the riders and their team was not one that concerned itself with small talk. Everyone had a job to do.

It had been decided ahead of time each of the men would concentrate his efforts on one equine. Choppy, with his Guanacaste horse sense and gentle touch, was best suited to Piper. That left Doc on Jack, the big vet taking care of the bigger mule.

Their movements had been rehearsed many times back in Lodi, and it really was like watching a race-car pit spring into action. The first thing they did was give Piper and Jack a good sponge down.

From there. it was going to be ice for the animals' legs. They bought it from a handsome, muscle-bound local who had made himself a fixture at the Tevis. He drove up to the vet checks—and anywhere else on the course with road access—in a 1950s era "Good Humor" truck and sold ice out of the back. Everyone knew where to find him because, even though the truck's speakers no longer worked, he'd call out "buck a bag," every so often. Folks called him Iceberg.

After the ice, it was water. Then, finally, feed—starting with some hay, just to get their stomachs up and working; going next to oats; and finishing with the bran-raisin mash Piper adored and Jack devoured. Lizzy called it raisin bran.

Miss Betty's job was to make sure each man had what they needed before they needed it, anticipating when they'd be coming for ice, when they'd want the sponge, when it was the right time for the mash.

The riders were expected to take care of themselves. For them, merely being out of the saddle was a treat in itself. Lizzy took a can of soda pop out of the cooler and a candy bar from the spread Miss Betty laid out. Then, dusty and exhausted, she flopped down on the shaded hay bale that Doc had recently vacated.

By that point, more than five hours into the race, the soda tasted like pure nectar, while the candy bar might as well have been manna. As she savored them, she rubbed her thighs, which were already sore and getting sorer.

One might have thought Cowgirl would have immediately joined her daughter in some well-deserved pampering. But she was standing with her fists jammed into her hips.

"Where's my husband?" she asked.

Miss Betty, Doc and Choppy were so busy tending to the animals, they either didn't hear her or didn't want to take the time to answer.

"Where's Cowboy?" Cowgirl demanded, a little louder.

"Don't go fussing at me, girl," Miss Betty said. "You came in earlier than I thought you would. I haven't had time to get him yet. He's in the main tent. I wanted to keep him out of the sun."

"Has he eaten?"

It was just like Cowgirl to think of Cowboy's care and feeding before her own.

"He's had breakfast," Miss Betty said. "We pulled off the road just outside Squaw Valley and took care of that. But he hasn't had lunch because it's not lunchtime yet, so don't start with me."

Cowgirl marched off without another word. She picked her way between the small aid stations that had been set up by the other support teams. Her red, pointy toed boots cut through the parts of the meadow grass that hadn't already been trampled down by feet and hooves.

When she found him, still sitting in his wheelchair in the main tent, his head was leaning to one side. There were tears leaking from his eyes.

Cowgirl put on her best smile.

"There's my handsome husband," she said, brightly.

She walked up to him and righted his head. She took a bandana out of her pocket and dabbed the side of his eyes until the moisture was gone. Then she appraised him. Not like a mother hen. But like a wife.

"Much better," she said.

She put her warm, trail-dusty hand to one of his cheeks, cupped it, then kissed the other one. Before his wreck, Cowboy used to tell people her lips felt like rose petals. Whether he could still feel their softness, no one knew.

"Missed you, baby," she said. "You have a good morning? Miss Betty said you had a nice breakfast."

Cowboy, of course, said nothing; because Cowboy never did.

It was, frankly, far beyond my understanding why she didn't resent the man, who left her not only with the sole responsibility of caring for their daughter, but also the burden of caring for him. I would have had some angry times, times when "why me" would have been the only question on my mind.

If those words ever slipped from Cowgirl's mouth in that order, no one was around to hear them. She never seemed to act like Cowboy was a burden, or even the "worse" in "for better or worse."

It was just her marriage and her life. And, yes, both had taken a turn on that one tragic night no one had anticipated. But once it did, she accepted it without complaint.

Some folks figured it was her faith, that the preacher's daughter leaned on a lifetime of her father's sermons and found solace in the word of God. Maybe that was part of it.

But I think a much greater part was simply that she had fallen in love with Cowboy a long, long time ago, back when he was the handsome young son of a rancher, the only boy in Lodi who was as gifted on horseback as she was, and the only student in the Lodi High School Class of 1965 who was her superior.

She fell deeply in love with him. His goal each day, which he borrowed from the song of a California boarding school he never actually went to, was "to do the best work in the world that we can do till the best we can do is all done." He applied this to his studies, his ranch work, everything in his life.

If you think that doesn't sound like something a young woman might be attracted to, then you don't know Cowgirl, who always prized practicality and good sense. People who knew her as a little girl say she turned forty on her tenth birthday.

And, yes, Cowboy was no longer capable of doing the kind of work he once did. Nor was he capable of much else. But it didn't change the fact that Cowgirl was still in love with him.

The rest of the world saw a wreck of a human being, a shell of a man in a wheelchair. Cowgirl still saw the comely rancher's son she had fallen in love with.

"All right, let's get you back with the team where you belong," she said. "There's work to do."

She started rolling him across the bumpy meadow. His chair turned out not to be as handy at slicing through the long grass as her pointy red boots. Cowgirl pushed him all the same, her powerful arms and thighs more than equal to the task.

"You would have been *so* proud of your daughter this morning," Cowgirl said. "There was some real technical stuff on that trail and she handled it like a true horsewoman. She's getting so, so...big. Sometimes I look at her and I just can't believe she's fourteen."

They rolled forward.

"Remember when we brought her home from the hospital? We had her swaddled in the well of the pickup and I don't think you went faster than twenty-five miles an hour the whole way home. We thought she was so fragile. It was like she was our little tea cup."

"Would you ever really have thought that someday she'd be riding the Tevis?

Did you?"

She pushed on. With each step, there was another pair of eyes staring at them. If a stunningly beautiful woman pushing her invalid husband in a wheelchair happened by you, you'd stare, too. If not at him, then certainly at her.

"Oh, of course you did," Cowgirl resumed, answering her own question. "You always knew she'd ride the Tevis someday. Damn, you always were just a little bit smarter!"

She laughed.

"But I'll tell you what, we've raised ourselves a beautiful, amazing, smart and wonderful girl. Together. We have. And she will be an extraordinary woman," Cowgirl smiled.

She was nearing her support team now, so she stopped talking. Cowgirl had told Wooly she talked to the man in the moon. Truth was, she talked to Cowboy. She said the things to him she never said to anyone else.

And Cowboy just sat in his chair. He was nothing if not also a good listener.

But as she spoke, more tears leaked from his eyes.

Cowboy's crying—and he did it all the time—was one of those behaviors the doctors simply wrote off.

They said it was a reflex. Like swallowing. Or kicking out his leg when you tapped his knee in just the right spot. They said that anyone who held their eyes wide open long enough would start crying, too. It was just one of those things a body knew how to do whether you wanted it to or not.

I think there really was something going on in that cracked-up head of his; that he could see his condition, and it overwhelmed him so much he couldn't help but weep.

Maybe it's just because I can so easily imagine him on that fateful night, at the Grand National Rodeo Championship. I can smell the rodeo clowns' grease paint, the popcorn and beer, the arena dirt, the hot breath of the crowd.

The event was held at the Cow Palace in San Francisco that year. There were 12,953 seats and every one of them was filled.

Cowgirl had finished with her part of the competition the day before. She was a star roper, a superior barrel racer, and unbeatable in cutting and reining. She won the all-around blue ribbon and that trailer, the one with "All-American Cowgirl 1977" in block letters. Back then, the lettering was shiny and new, not peeling and cracking.

It was now Cowboy's turn to win the bull riding. There had never been husband-and-wife champions before. The 12,953 spectators were cheering for it—not just because it was history, but because Cowboy and Cowgirl were so dashing together, it was hard not to root for them.

Grand National finals required three rides on three

different bulls, spaced over three nights. Each ride had to last at least eight seconds in order to be scored. Some of the best riders from all around North America hadn't made it through the first two rounds.

And now, for the third round, they were using some of the biggest, baddest bulls on the planet, an assortment of Brahmans as violent as they were strong. There was a reason they were known as eliminators.

The eliminator Cowboy had drawn was named Ambush, an angry chunk of bull meat that didn't take kindly to anyone trying to hop on his back. He was broad in the chest but lighter in the flanks. It was a dangerous combination—power in the front but flexibility in the rear—because it rendered an animal capable of generating a tremendous amount of torque.

Cowboy told himself he was ready for whatever Ambush could dish out, right down to the smallest details. The bull rope was one of Choppy's finest. The red snap shirt he wore was one Cowgirl had bought him, and it matched his lucky fringed chaps. His spotless, tan Stetson was a gift from his daughter, and she had kissed it before he put it on.

Why a 140-pound cowboy feels protected from an eighteen hundred pound bull by a few superstitious talismans is a psychology beyond explanation. Unless the explanation is that bull riders are crazy.

Cowgirl had splurged on ringside seats. Her tiny clone, six-year-old Lizzy, was there at her side. She was now old enough to recognize this was a big deal and that her Daddy was doing something pretty special. And everyone in the family was realizing that Cowboy, who was now thirty—positively geriatric for a bull rider—might not have too many more chances to do this.

There was a special buzz in the air as Cowboy headed to the chute for his third ride. It was the history. It was the radiance that Cowgirl brought to the proceeding. But it was also the bull, who added an energy all his own to the event.

Cowboy always believed in spending a few minutes studying a bull before he rode it. He felt like he could get a sense of the beast's tendencies. Was it going to be a head-down spinner? A straight ahead bucker? What moves might it try?

The thing that struck Cowboy about this bull was that it seemed to have spikes in its blood. It shuffled and pawed and almost growled in the chute. Cowboy was thinking he had never ridden a bull that seemed so full of wrath.

There was a reason for that, of course. The bull had an abscess just behind its front left leg, where a cactus spine had broken off five days before. The wound was now swollen, pussy, and exceptionally tender. It was also in the exact spot where the flank strap looped around. When the strap was cinched tightly, it squeezed the abscess, sending jolts of pain through the bull, making an animal that had already been bred to be mean even more vicious.

The Cow Palace had a veterinarian on hand to check out all the bulls for just such trouble. The vet on duty that night had simply missed the abscess.

So no one knew, as Cowboy approached the chute, that he was walking toward a loaded bovine grenade. He simply swung his legs over the rail and tried to tell himself this was just one more ride in a career full of them.

Cowboy had often told Cowgirl about this moment, about the instant right before he seized the rope and straddled the bull. He admitted he was always nervous—he scarcely would have been human if he wasn't.

It wasn't because he was afraid of getting hurt. That thought, ironically enough, never entered his mind. It was the fear of the unknown. You can never quite guess what nine-tenths of a ton of infuriated bull is going to do next, and eight seconds can be a hellaciously long time to let him do it.

The other thing he always told Cowgirl about this

moment was that while it terrified him, it was also a time in his life when he felt most alive.

So there he was, feeling all that fear, dread, and exhilaration. He looked one last time at Cowgirl and Lizzy—"my blondies," he called them—and tipped that spotless Stetson of his.

He had it all planned out: how he would survive those eight wild seconds, then drop the rope and land with his feet firmly in the Cow Palace dirt. The crowd would roar its adoration as he waved at his blondies. He'd collect his $20,000 winner's check and—he hadn't told Cowgirl this part yet—he'd call it a career.

Four Grand National championships was enough for anyone. He had decided it was time to put their future dreams into place that he and Cowgirl had always talked about. They'd take their earnings from the rodeo circuit and plow most of it into a ranch of their own, with just enough left over for three fast Arabs that would allow them to ride the Tevis.

It was all out there for him.

He settled onto the bull's back, feeling all that aggression coursing underneath him, and clamped his gloved hand tightly on the bull rope.

The chute gatekeeper asked, "Ready?"

Cowboy nodded.

The horn sounded. The chute door open. The bull charged out into the arena.

Instantly, the volume in the Cow Palace tripled. The bull landed a furious kick as the door was closing, but Cowboy was ready for it.

There's a saying in bull riding that you don't ride the bull, you ride the buck. Cowboy was a master at it. He let his upper body flow with the undulations while his lower body stayed rock firm. There's another saying in bull riding—"Lose your feet, lose your seat"—that Cowboy paid special attention to. It's what made him a national champion so many times over.

Ambush was a spinner, just as Cowboy thought. So he was ready for the bull's early moves. It was bolting and twisting and dipping and straining, and Cowboy just kept his free hand high and let himself get whipped in circles for one second, two seconds, three seconds. Everything was working exactly the way he thought it would. Four seconds. Five seconds.

And then came the sixth second, when the spinner suddenly turned into a bucker. And his first effort was not any run-of-the-mill buck. Just at the moment Cowboy was ever so slightly off-center from the last spin—maybe just a very few inches—the bull coiled every muscle grouping in its massive body and unleashed a kick that sent its hind hooves twelve feet in the air.

Cowboy lurched forward. Those extra few inches he was off balance multiplied exponentially, and suddenly the bull had leverage like he never had before. Cowboy's feet, those feet that were so key to everything, went wide.

Once his lower body was unmoored, his upper body followed with breathtaking speed. The bull rope was ripped from his right hand and now he was completely loose.

He catapulted over the bull's horns and landed right in front of the animal, which was just about the worst place possible. The rodeo clowns dashed out to do their job, but this was not a bull that was going to be distracted. It was raging with pain and fury at the man who had climbed on his back and now it was plowing for revenge.

Ambush aimed his horns for the back of Cowboy's red shirt, then scooped up the garment and its inhabitant and flipped it ten feet in the air, as effortlessly as tossing a fork full of hay.

Cowboy sailed in the air, then landed hard on the dirt. But Ambush wasn't done. The last thing Cowboy saw—before the seven weeks of darkness that were to follow—were the bull's front hooves crashing down on his head.

Chapter

11

Hitch

ONCE PIPER AND JACK WERE TAKEN CARE OF—sponged and cooled, fed and watered—the support team settled in to hear about the morning.

Cowgirl positioned her husband in the middle of everyone so he could hear about crotchety old Vernon Puce, about Jack hauling Wooly up Cougar Rock, about Wooly singing Lizzy across Elephant Trunk.

As the stories were exchanged, Cowgirl had taken a pinch of Skoal Long Cut—Cowboy's favorite—and worked it around between his cheek and gum. It was something she did just about every day, usually in the morning, right after she put on his old boots.

Anyone watching from a nearby camp would have probably thought it was quite odd to see a woman's hand rooting around in her paralyzed husband's mouth. Cowgirl swore it settled him down, that she could see the gratitude in his eyes when that little jolt of nicotine hit his bloodstream.

Cowgirl had taken off her red snap shirt by that point. Underneath, she wore a simple white tank top that showed off her arms, which were tanned like oak trees and every bit as solid, with veins that popped out on both the forearms and biceps. They were arms that flexed all day, lifting water buckets, hay bales, and her husband's withered body. At night, they were tender arms that held and comforted. If Cowboy had any room left in his head for a thought, I'm sure an appreciation for those magnificent arms would have been one.

When she thought he had enough dip, she fished it out of his mouth and kissed him on the forehead. Like Miss Betty, she was trying to ignore just how ashen his skin was growing.

For her part, Miss Betty had turned her attention away from Cowboy and the equines and was mothering up Lizzy instead. First, she gave the girl a wet washcloth, so she could wipe away at least some of the thirty-four miles worth of dust that had accumulated on her. Then the old nurse started pestering the girl about switching from soda pop to water, because hydration was just as important for the riders as it was for the mounts, and about putting down the candy bars and picking up a turkey sandwich, because it would give her more energy for later.

Lizzy gave in to both demands.

Choppy was still working on the animals. During his examination of their hooves, he had noticed that one of Jack's shoes had lost two nails and was loose. So he set about fixing that.

Next he climbed on Piper's back. Arabs typically have long, flowing manes, and Piper was no different. Choppy began braiding it, knowing it would help her beat the heat that was surely coming.

Doc Jenson had returned to one of the hay bales. But once Cowgirl was done administering her husband's daily dose of tobacco, Doc pulled himself up and approached her.

The relationship between Doc and Cowgirl was one that takes some explaining. He was, after all, the vet who missed the abscess on the bull. And for that reason, a lot of folks felt she should have been furious at him. Forever.

But that never even seemed to occur to Cowgirl.

It was no one's fault, she would say. *Bull riding is a dangerous sport. My husband knew the risks.*

Personally, I have a hard time blaming Doc, too. A bull is a huge animal, and it doesn't exactly stand around and let a veterinarian take his time poking and prodding. Some folks said it was because of Doc's size that he was unable to get beneath the bull for a good look. But that wound was located in a place no one could have seen. It really could have happened to anyone.

Doc never saw it that way. He told anyone who would listen it was his fault, then made all kinds of attempts to set things right. He even offered to testify against himself in a malpractice suit. When Cowgirl declined to sue, he offered her money, straight up. She refused to accept it.

That wasn't good enough for Doc, who felt the weight of his mistake like a lead yoke. That bull's abscess eventually healed. It's fair to say Doc never did.

And yet, in his efforts to flog himself for his mistake, Cowgirl saw his genuine remorse. And she wanted him to realize she truly bore him no malice.

Somehow, out of that, they became friends. Doc kept coming around, trying to convince her to let him do this or that for her, and she kept insisting she didn't want anything from him.

After a while, when she saw he wasn't going to give up, they reached the unofficial and unspoken arrangement that he serve up, a lifetime supply of free veterinary care. She accepted simply because she knew it didn't cost him much but his time and a few medications now and again.

His participation on her Tevis crew was a natural outcropping of that. Truly, no one knew Jack or Piper better than Doc. He had been their personal veterinarian from the moment they entered Cowgirl's barn.

He knew Cowgirl pretty well, too. And he knew he had

yet another thing to set right. So once she was done with her wifely duties, he rambled over toward her and cleared his throat.

"Got a moment?" he asked.

"Yep."

Doc placed a fatherly hand on her shoulder. "I'm sorry for...for saying what I did before. I was out of line, just something that slipped out in the heat of the moment with all of us there. I've just never seen him have one of those seizures and...I guess I was at a loss, except for the wrong words."

"It's okay. Without you there…I don't want to think how that would have gone. Thanks."

Doc just shook his head.

She let that rest.

"You got a second for some horse and mule talk?" Doc asked.

"Sure."

"I checked out both the animals from tip to tail. Piper is looking good. Real good. I could tell from the way she trotted up here that she was feeling okay. But having really examined her, I can tell you she's better than okay. It's like she knows this is what she was born for."

"But?" Cowgirl said, because the look on Doc's face told her there was a "but" coming.

"But I'm concerned about Jack," Doc said. "He's looking fine right now, don't get me wrong. But a mule is not an Arab. He's not bred to run the way she is. As this race goes on, Piper is going to want to *go*. And she'll have the pep in her legs to do it, too. I don't know if Jack is going to be able to keep up."

"He's going to want to, though. You know how it is with those two."

"I know it. Believe me, I know. That's why I'm telling you this. You're going to have to hold Piper back if you want

Jack to finish."

"I'm doing my best," she said.

"I know you are," he said. "And I know there's a lot of race left. I just...Piper is looking so strong. All that training you've done has really paid off."

"Jack's been with her every step of it, you know."

"I know," he said.

Then he smiled a little. He had been there as head of the Tevis Vet Committee for every one of Cowgirl's six failed attempts and had felt her pain right along with her. This was now almost as much his quest as it was hers, and the two of them had spent many a winter night sharing coffee and talking about how things would be done differently on a future, long-off August day.

"You're actually a little ahead of schedule right now," he said, allowing the grin to grow. "I don't want to jinx you, but I think this could be the year."

She glanced toward Cowboy.

"I sure hope so," she said. "I sure hope so."

As the hour hold came to an end, something else was definitely beginning: a rift between Lizzy and the rest of the team. It was small, for now. But there was no question it was there. Everyone else was quite eager to get back on the trail. Cowgirl had this little bounce in her stride. She had kept herself moving during the break, not allowing her body to get stiff. Her thighs had the advantage of countless more thousands of hours of riding time, and they weren't but a little bit fatigued.

Piper was ready to go, too. She whinnied and snorted as Doc put her saddle on, knowing full well this meant she'd get to run more. Jack was silent, as usual, though he was clearly ready for more work.

But there was no doubt Lizzy was not. For her, the hour

had gone too fast. She had relished the time out of the saddle even more than she did her candy bars. And now she wasn't terribly keen to continue.

She wasn't saying anything—being Cowgirl's daughter made her predisposed not to whine—but her discomfort was plain to anyone who looked at her. The lactic acid that had built up in her legs during the rest time made it painful to stand and walk. Or hobble, as was the case. And no amount of rubbing was going to help.

As she hoisted herself up on Jack, she was wincing. And the rest of the team knew, even though she was suffering in silence, that she wasn't as keen to continue as the rest.

It was Choppy who actually did something about it.

"*Momentito*," he announced.

He hustled over to a leather satchel that was leaning against one of the hay bales. He opened the flap and lifted out a small brown figure.

"I meant to give this to you at the start, I just forgot," Choppy said from over his shoulder.

Then he turned to face Lizzy.

"Jenny!" she said, suddenly beaming at her tiny leather mule.

"She wouldn't want to miss this adventure, you know?"

"Of course not."

"Did I ever tell you about the time Jenny ran the Tevis?" Choppy said.

"No, I don't think I ever heard that one," Lizzy said, smiling.

"*Si*. She ran and she ran and she ran. And, every time things got hard, her rider gave her a little pat because she knew it would bring her good luck. And then Jenny and all her friends made it to the finish line with time to spare, and they all got beautiful belt buckles. The end."

He pretended to make the mule run as he spoke. As he finished, he smiled, flashing his gold tooth.

"I like that story," Lizzy said.

"Okay, now give her a little pat."

Lizzy did as she was told.

"Good," Choppy replied, carefully slipping Jenny the Mule into her saddlebag. "Now go make the story come true."

Coming out of Robinson Flat, there's a small climb up to the top of a little rise called Cavanaugh Ridge.

It's nothing for the horses. And the rookie riders just fly by it, not understanding its significance. But the veteran riders know it's one of the most pivotal points of the Tevis, a time when they're going to learn just how much punishment they're really in for.

Because it's there, at the top of Cavanaugh Ridge, at about 11:30 in the morning—which is when Cowgirl and Lizzy reached it—that you get your first real indicator of how hot it's going to be.

If there's a little bit of a breeze coming from the west, hitting you in the face as you crest that ridge, then you know your ride might not be too bad. It'll be in the nineties, of course, because it gets into the nineties nearly every day during the summer in the Sierra Nevada, particularly at the bottom of the valleys. But that breeze, which has come cool and fresh off the distant Pacific and somehow mustered the strength to make it that far inland, will stir the air just enough to keep things manageable.

If there's no breeze, you know you're in for trouble.

No breeze means the Sierra Nevada is about to turn into a blast oven with nothing to stop temperatures as they soar to a hundred degrees and beyond. No breeze means the horses can't keep water in them, no matter how much they drink. No breeze means you can absolutely guarantee that the majority of the 199 competitors who started the race in

Squaw Valley won't be making it to Auburn in time to collect their buckles.

Cowgirl had done the Tevis enough times to know what Cavanaugh Ridge meant. As she neared the top, she slowed Piper to a walk, then to a stop.

"What's up, Mom?" Lizzy asked.

Cowgirl didn't respond. She was trying to be mindful of her face, which had a sheen of sweat on it. She was yearning to feel that little tingle that told her the breeze was going to be their constant friend throughout the worst of the afternoon heat.

Because she knew how well Piper was doing. And she knew Jack could compensate with willpower for what he lacked in leg speed. The Tevis still had a lot of punishment to dish out at them, sure. But a breeze would tell her they had a decent chance of surviving it.

A breeze just might bring them a buckle.

"Mom, what's going on?" Lizzy said.

"Nothing, dear," Cowgirl said.

Cowgirl gave Piper a squeeze and they continued up on over the ridge, through air that was as deadly still as the inside of a coffin.

Chapter

12

The Point

COMING OFF THE RIDGE, they were able to get into a good rhythm. It's a gentle downhill slope at that point, and they were once again on wide logging paths that allowed them to go whatever speed they pleased and pass other horses at will.

It's not that Cowgirl was completely ignoring Doc's warning. But she knew Piper and Jack even better than he did. And while Doc had been to veterinary school and understood horses' anatomy, Cowgirl had been to what might be called pasture school, and therefore had a better understanding of horses' behavior. She was more in tune with them on a metaphysical level.

Her father, a Methodist minister, first put her on a Shetland pony named Shoofly when she was not more than two-and-a-half years old. She was immediately hooked. I'm not sure another day of her childhood passed that she wasn't on a horse's back for at least a little while.

While her father's calling had taken them to Lodi, an agriculturally industrial town in west central California, he and his wife were originally from San Francisco. He was eventually able to win over the local populace though he was at first considered with suspicion, as city types often are in a small town.

There was always a bit of a push and pull when it came to Cowgirl and whether her upbringing would be more city or country. Her mother was refined and educated. She exposed her daughter to the classics of literature, art and music. And there was at least a half-hour of music practice for Cowgirl each day, along with a poem to read.

But, ultimately, while Cowgirl minded her citified mother, the country won out. They lived on the outskirts of town in a small house that had been given to the church many years before. Their nearest neighbor—basically, their only neighbor—was the man who owned the Shetland pony, and twenty-odd head of horses beyond that.

There weren't any other kids out that way, so Cowgirl made friends with the horses instead. When she wasn't riding them, she'd spend hours just watching them, earning credits at pasture school.

That's where she really got to know them, where she would see little glimpses of the wild horse that's still alive and well inside the domesticated animal. It's a part of them that only comes out when they're in a pasture that's large enough to mimic the broad plains of their ancestors. That's where they establish that pecking order that is so critical for any herd.

Cowgirl came to recognize that Arabs mostly do this through running games. You'll watch them trying to egg each other on, making these little charges at each other, challenging each other to a race. As soon as one of them takes off, they all go. The last one still running is considered the winner.

They only do it when they think no one is watching. And Cowgirl, a little pipsqueak in blond pigtails, wasn't big enough for them to take much notice of her. She got to be a silent witness to their displays of horsiness. Few others understood the animals better than she did.

After enough time, those horses started to think of her as

one of the herd. And she learned both how to be a member of the herd, when that suited her, but also how to be the alpha as was sometimes needed.

When she was old enough and strong enough, she started working for the neighbor, who had already seen the passion she had for the animals. Soon enough, Cowgirl was taking care of horses before and after school each day. The neighbor gave her a bit of money in exchange for her work. But, for Cowgirl, it was clear most of the compensation wasn't monetary.

Cowgirl was about fourteen—Lizzy's age—when the neighbor added two mules to his stock. That's when she came to appreciate the intelligence and ability of those animals. It gave her a good eye, years later, when it came time to buy Jack. She could see his special qualities, particularly how calm he was. She knew it would make him perfect for her daughter.

As for Piper, well, just about anyone could see what a tremendous athlete she was. But it took someone with Cowgirl's touch—and Jack's calming influence—to unlock her gifts.

So Cowgirl knew, what potential her team had. And, Doc's warnings and the ominous portents of Cavanaugh Ridge aside, she was confident in her team as they began putting some serious miles behind them, even as the day heated up every bit as much as she knew it would.

She was confident in the equine members of her team.

The other human member was more of an open question.

After Dusty Corners, which is nothing more than a quick water stop, the trail is a bit rocky, but otherwise unremarkable. After so many miles, you can be lulled into a sense of complacency, so much so that the next Tevis obstacle sneaks up and startles the hell out of you.

Cowgirl knew full well what was coming, of course. Maybe she was hoping Lizzy would just sail past it or grit through it or what have you. Sometimes rearing a teenager and handling the thorniest parts of the Tevis are sort of like the same thing. You're aware of the possible perils, of course. You're just hoping if you don't make a big deal out of it, the child won't get caught up in them.

Fact is, for someone as fearful of heights as Lizzy, there is no more dreadful section of the Tevis than the canyon that comes not long after Dusty Corners.

Out of seemingly nowhere, the wide, gentle trail narrows down to a width no greater than a long bar table turned the skinny way. On your left is a wall of rock. On your right is a sheer, thousand-foot drop into the American River. You'd swear, if you spit, it would land in the water.

There are several bends where you can't even tell there's a trail in front of you. All you can see is your horse's nose, hanging out over the abyss.

There's a reason this part of the trail has gotten the name Pucker Point.

As bad as Elephant Trunk is, Tevis veterans will tell you Pucker Point is ten times worse. Especially with no Wooly to sing you over it. And Lizzy was just riding along, hot, dusty but otherwise happy, when she suddenly realized what was coming.

And unlike Elephant Trunk, where she didn't know how bad it was going to get until it was already too late, this time she knew.

"Wait, is *that* the trail?" she asked, bringing Jack to a sudden halt. She was pointing a shaky hand toward the side of the cliff.

"Yep," said Cowgirl, trying to play it off like it wasn't all that bad.

It didn't work.

"Uh-uh. No way," Lizzy said. "I'm not doing it."

Cowgirl circled Piper around so she could look at her daughter.

"I can't," Lizzy said, trying to end the debate before it began. "I just can't."

"Nonsense. You did fine with Elephant Trunk."

"I was not *fine*, Mom. I nearly passed out."

"Well, okay. But you still made it over in one piece."

"No I...look, I can't do it again, okay? There's just...it's just not happening."

"Jack can get you over with no trouble," Cowgirl insisted. "He'll follow Piper and not think twice. You can close your eyes if you like."

Lizzy was already shaking her head. As if to make it clear this was as far as she planned to go, she dismounted. "You can go on without me. I'll just head back to Robinson Flat. I'll hitch a ride with the riders whose cards got pulled. I'll be fine. I'll be there in Auburn to cheer you on at the finish. You and Piper can go faster without me and Jack to slow you down anyway."

Cowgirl studied her daughter. Truth was, Piper wouldn't go another step without Jack by her side. He was her courage, her comfort animal. Absent his presence, she'd probably go back to being that nervous wreck of a horse who got disqualified at the first vet check the year before.

But to Cowgirl, that was the lesser issue. The larger one was that she didn't want her fourteen-year-old daughter riding off into the wilderness alone.

There was also, somewhere in Cowgirl, a stubborn refusal to allow their Tevis to end like this. Cowgirl could have accepted having to pack it in because one of the animals came up lame, or because a vet decided they weren't fit to continue, or because she or her daughter got sick or injured.

But not this.

She had now been mothering long enough—observing her daughter in the pasture, you could say—that she knew making demands wouldn't work. Lizzy had her shoulders hunched, her feet set, and a certain look about her, like a diamondback that's been backed into a corner and is waiting to strike at anything that moves.

So Cowgirl hopped off Piper, dropped the reins, and approached, so it wouldn't seem like she was issuing edicts from on high.

"You can quit if you want," she said. "But you're going to have to listen to your mother tell you one story first. It's about your Dad. Do you want to hear it?"

If anything was going to lure Lizzy out of her defensive stance, this was it. Cowgirl almost never told stories about Lizzy's father.

Lizzy just shifted her weight, saying nothing. It was unclear if she would take the bait.

"Well, are you going to hear me out or not?" Cowgirl asked. "I haven't got all day."

Lizzy bit her lower lip for a moment or two of deliberation. But, ultimately, even a tidbit of talk about her father was too good to refuse. Her shoulders relaxed. Just a little.

"Okay," Lizzy allowed.

"All right. So this was maybe four months after the accident? Your father had been in the hospital for the first three months, mind you. He had been in that coma and then he came out of it and he was...well, he was pretty much like he is now. Are you sure you want me to tell you this?"

Lizzy had already been nibbling at the bait. This was Cowgirl getting her to swallow it whole while setting the hook.

"Yeah, yeah. Keep going."

"Well, okay. After three months in the hospital, the doctors finally said there was nothing more they could do. I think the hospital knew our savings were just about gone and we weren't going to be able to pay our bills if we stayed much longer. Anyhow, they said I should hire some nursing help and take care of your father at home. I asked Choppy to build the wheelchair ramp for us. So home we went.

"We couldn't afford nursing help, of course. But I thought...well, I don't know what I was thinking. I really thought I'd be able to handle you and your father by myself. I told myself I was young and tough and strong and I could do anything."

She stopped and shook her head. Lizzy had taken a few steps closer.

"Turns out, I was simply wrong," Cowgirl continued. "I was trying to handle your father's every need and yours as well, without any help at all. He was still in pretty rough shape after the accident and we didn't have a routine down then like we do now. I was also trying to make pies to sell, because I knew we needed to get money coming in somehow. After a month of that, I had run myself ragged. Every night I would just sob because I had exhausted myself making it through the day, and I didn't think I'd be able to do it again the next one.

"And then, one morning, there was a knock at the door. You were at school."

Cowgirl's eyes were set far in the distance. "I went to answer it, and there was this grizzled woman standing there. She was dressed in green nurse's scrubs and she was squinting at me real hard. I don't even want to think about what she was seeing. I probably hadn't showered in four days at that point. My hair was a mess. I had dirt under my nails and stains on my shirt and deep circles under my eyes. To top it off, there was a sink full of dishes and unfolded laundry all over the house.

"Anyway, this woman said she had heard about me and she was there to help. And I told her thank you, but I was flat broke and couldn't afford to pay her. And she said that wasn't necessary. She also told me about this thing called the Cowboy Up Foundation and how they were going to send me a check every month so I didn't have to worry about money quite so much."

"It was Miss Betty, wasn't it," Lizzy said. "The old woman was Miss Betty."

"It was, yes. And knowing what I know now, I wonder how it was she hid her wings underneath those scrubs, because she was an absolute angel, come to save me. To save us. But do you know what I said to her back then?"

"What?"

"I told her no thank you. I told her we were fine and that I couldn't accept her help or her charity. I was literally on the brink of cracking into a thousand pieces, but I was turning her away. And she just fixed me with one of her Miss Betty looks and said, 'Girl, don't be a damn fool. Everyone needs help sometimes.'

"And, just at that moment, your father let out a loud moan from the next room. His legs had cramped." And Miss Betty said, "Sounds like your husband needs you. Now get out of my way and invite me in. I'm going to tidy this place up while you tend to your man, and then we can talk. "

Cowgirl smiled and shook her head. "I just stood there in the doorway for another moment or two. Then your father moaned again, and I realized I didn't have a choice. There was no way I was going to make it on my own. I had to accept her help or I was going to just break apart, and then we'd be in real trouble."

Lizzy was nodding, and Cowgirl closed the gap between them. She put both hands on Lizzy's shoulders. Their matching sapphire eyes locked on each other.

"You're strong and stubborn like me," Cowgirl said. "You don't want to accept anyone's help. I get that. And sometimes stubborn is the best thing we have going for us in this world. But sometimes you have to allow yourself to trust others. It's the only way to make it through.

"Trust Jack. The next bad step that mule takes will be

his first. He'll get you out and around that point without any trouble."

For a moment, Lizzy didn't move. Then her chin dipped ever so slightly before going back up. She repeated the movement twice more.

It was a nod—almost imperceptible, yes. But a nod nevertheless.

"Okay, Mom," she said.

And then she put one foot in the left stirrup and swung back up on big Jack, who continued on like he didn't know what all the fuss was about. He took her out around Pucker Point, one plodding step after another, the deathly drop to the American River not giving him a second's pause.

And Lizzy, she just buried her face in his mane and clung to his neck, keeping her eyes closed the whole way.

Chapter

13

Last Chance

NOT LONG AFTER PUCKER POINT is a gate-and-go situated in a gold-mining ghost town known as Last Chance.

Nowadays, Last Chance is so empty I think even the ghosts have given up on it. Tevis folks—and a few hardy trail riders—are pretty much the only people who ever wander through the place.

But during the height of the gold rush in the mid-1800's, thousands of miners passed through the town each year. It was a thriving place, with a saloon, a hotel, a hardware store and a blacksmith shop, everything a man needed to fortify himself so he could continue pulling precious ore from the nearby hills. It was a place where fortunes were made and lost, where the Wild West was at its wildest, where the legends that created the American spirit were both incubated and born.

Now, all that's left are a few rusted door hinges and bits of tools, a small shack, and a cemetery.

For Tevis riders, Last Chance marks the midpoint of the race, which is a daunting thing if you think about it too long. Fifty miles is a wearying distance to travel on a horse. Even the leaders don't reach Last Chance until at least 12:30 in the afternoon. For middle-of-the-packers like Cowgirl and

Lizzy, it was more like 1:30—nearly eight-and-a-half hours after they began.

It can be downright disheartening to think you have another fifty miles and at least eight-and-a-half hours to go—and probably longer, since the deepest canyons are still to come.

Piper and Jack, who had already passed through the pulse check, were now taking advantage of some of the water and feed brought in by the volunteers. Cowgirl knew how important it was for them to eat as much as they wanted, and she wasn't going to rush them.

In an effort to pass the time—and keep Lizzy distracted from just how much still lay ahead—Cowgirl took her on a little tour of Last Chance and told her how it got its name.

The legend is that the area was so rich with gold deposits, and the first miners to reach it were so fevered to collect it all before anyone else arrived, they stayed too long—long past when their supplies and provisions had run out.

With starvation threatening, they were down to one bullet. A miner grabbed his rifle and announced that bullet was their "last chance" for a grub stake. He went out into the forest and returned with a large buck. It allowed the miners to keep prospecting—and eating. They called their camp Last Chance in honor of that buck, and the town that built up around it kept the name.

Lizzy listened thoughtfully, swatting occasionally at one of the mosquitoes that swarmed Last Chance, as Cowgirl retold the history, then pointed out the sunken spots in the pine straw that marked where there was once a house cellar.

"So there were really thousands of people here every year?" Lizzy asked.

"Yep," Cowgirl said.

"Living their lives and having their dreams?"

"Living and dying and everything in between," Cowgirl confirmed.

"And now it's gone."

"Yep."

Lizzy surveyed the scant ruins. Here and there, she could see what might have been a hinge, or a coffee pot, or a stovepipe—all badly rusted. In a few more decades, the forest would reclaim them.

"Everything in this world comes to an end, you know. Everything has a finish line," Cowgirl said. "Everything that lives, dies. Everything built by humans eventually crumbles. Everything nature creates is sooner or later devoured by time and decay."

It was the kind of expansive thinking Lizzy never heard coming from her mother. There was just seldom time, in their daily existence, for much philosophy. And I think it's fair to say, right then, Lizzy was aware there were some nerve endings exposed on her mother and wanted to take advantage of them before they got covered up again.

"Would you have said that before Daddy got hurt?" Lizzy asked. "Or did you only start thinking that way after?"

Cowgirl took a swipe at a mosquito, then walked out into the sunshine, where they were less legion. She squinted at the brightness.

"I'm sure that's what a lot of people would believe," she said.

"What do you mean?"

Cowgirl took a deep breath and let it go slowly.

"Oh, Lizzy."

"What?"

Cowgirl seemed to be making up her mind about whether she should even start. Then she saw something in her daughter. It was her earnestness, yes. But it was also the woman in her, peeking out from under the girl. And I think Cowgirl realized the woman in her daughter needed—and deserved—another woman talking straight to her.

"Your father and I...we were...I'm not saying this to be

boastful, it's just the truth. We were really quite something as a couple. We were sharing our future hopes and living out our joy and dream. We were traveling the country from one rodeo to the next, pulling checks almost every week. We had all the money we needed. We were healthy and young and so very, very happy. And then, after the wreck, it looked like tragedy beyond repair to a lot of people. But I never saw it that way."

"Why not?"

"Because, to me, happiness has always been fleeting. If I eat an ice cream cone, I'll be happy. If I go on a nice trail ride with Piper and Jack, I'll be happy. But those things naturally come to an end. Like these buildings and this town. In due time, even if it's a long time, they're gone."

Lizzy's brow was furrowed. She wasn't liking the sound of a world where everything was transitory.

"So no one can ever be happy for longer than just a little while?" she asked.

"All you can do is cherish happiness while it lasts. You either finish the ice cream or it melts," Cowgirl said.

"Geez, Mom. That sucks."

"It does if all you focus on is happiness. But happiness is not the only goal. There are other things in this life that don't end and that aren't fleeting. That's what people have never understood about your father and me. True, we're not happy like we once were. But we still have joy and hope. Joy and hope feed dreams.

Then Cowgirl paused and looked towards the scrub-laced ridge at the edge of town and wistfully said,

"Hope is that thing with feathers-
That perches in the soul-
And sings the tune without the words-
And never stops-at all. "

"Mom," surprised that more of Cowgirl's inside was oozing out, Lizzy asked, "And where did that come from?"

"My favorite poet, Emily Dickinson, wrote those words about the time this town was alive with hopes and dreams and the joy of finding gold." She paused then continued, "And your Dad and I have love. Love lasts. And we have the joy of all our hard work and all we accomplished. No bull wreck can take that away."

Cowgirl smiled.

"Yeah, but...but...I mean, you lost your dream."

"Dreams have a way of changing, dear. And your Dad and I have the joy in dreams that did not change. Like having you as our daughter," Cowgirl said.

Lizzy didn't immediately reply. She returned to scanning the outline of what had once been a bustling main street, now overgrown with grassy weeds.

Eventually she said, "So this is Last Chance."

Saying the words out loud made a thought appear in her head: that this was her Dad's last chance, too. His last chance to see them ride the Tevis. His last chance to see them win a buckle. His last chance to be a part—even a small part—of the race he loved so much. And then he, too, would be gone. Like the buildings. Like the town. Like everything else in a world where nothing was permanent.

Suddenly, Lizzy was wiping tears from her eyes with her hand, the one that didn't have the splint on it.

"What is it, dear?" Cowgirl asked.

Lizzy just shook her head. She didn't want to say it. No matter how expansive a mood Cowgirl was in, Lizzy knew there were certain things she didn't want to hear.

"Nothing, Momma," she choked out, finally. "It's just... my finger hurts."

She wiped more tears. "My finger hurts and I miss

playing my violin. That's all."

That wasn't it, of course. But Cowgirl took a long look at her daughter, then reached out with one of those strong, tanned, oaken arms and wrapped it around Lizzy's shoulder.

"I know, baby girl," Cowgirl said. "I know."

The animals were almost done eating. And Cowgirl and Lizzy probably should have been getting ready so they could get back on the trail. But they just stood together for a little while, there in the ghost town known as Last Chance.

There was no music playing, of course. There probably hadn't been music there in ninety years, since the last of the town's inhabitants finally died off.

But if there had been music, I know for certain it would have been *Praeludium and Allegro*, composed a long time ago by an Austrian named Fritz Kreisler.

I'm not much for classical music—unless you're talking about Emmylou Harris or Linda Ronstadt. If I had never come across Cowgirl or Lizzy, I'd have probably told you a fellow named Kreisler made cars for a living.

But, no, he made music. Absolutely beautiful music. And Lizzy had spent most of her eighth grade year mastering *Praeludium and Allegro*, practicing it hour after endless hour until the violin fingerings were a part of her soul.

I have listened to *Praeludium and Allegro*. It is a powerful piece, one that stirs a certain something in your heart, even if violin music is not your thing, even if you don't know Kreisler from Chrysler.

It starts off with a big climb, just like the Tevis itself. Then it gets quite tricky, and you can't believe that simple combination—a few tight strings, a wooden box, a bow and a human's fingers—can make sounds that complex. It flows and it waves and it dodges. Then there's a really fast section, where you can imagine a horse at a brisk canter through a sharply scented pine forest.

Then the finish is so breathtaking, it puts this charge into your soul, and then it takes all those emotions it's been building in you and launches them across the finish line.

Folks said that when Lizzy played that piece, she brought a certain something extra to it, the way great artists do. I think it was hope, which had been in short supply in her life for far too long.

Praeludium and Allegro was going to be her audition song for the San Francisco School of Music, a prestigious school that attracted the finest young musicians in the country. She had already figured out that this was her entree into the world of professional violin and, perhaps, more importantly, out of Lodi.

The little town had always been too small for Lizzy, who had a lot of her grandmother in her and perhaps not as much of her mother, at least when it came to that city-or-country sensibility. I think it's also fair to say that some of her wanderlust was inspired by the fact that staying in Lodi meant sitting around in that too-quiet house and watching her father fade away.

All spring, she had been practicing *Praeludium* with the kind of intensity her father once brought to bull riding. She practiced so hard she kept wearing out violin bows. Knowing the bows were made of horse tail hair, Choppy tried to fix one of the broken bows with fine white strands from Piper's tail, using some jerry-rigged equipment instead of the stringing machine the professionals use.

It didn't really work. But Lizzy appreciated it all the same. It made her mastery of *Praeludium and Allegro* feel like a family effort.

And then came one Saturday in late May, a month before the audition and two months before the Tevis.

Cowgirl and Lizzy were taking every opportunity they could to go on long rides at that point, even when their schedule didn't necessarily allow for them. Cowgirl was in the kitchen, finishing up the last of the pies for a big order—Sunday being a day that folks like to eat a lot of pie. She had asked Lizzy to take Piper and Jack out of the barn and tack them up so they could get out on the trail before it got too late.

Lizzy was used to handling Jack, of course. He was her mule. But she had never taken Piper out of the barn before. That was always Cowgirl's job.

As you may know, horses can all be trained a little differently when it comes to certain things such as in tying. Some horses are schooled to simply stand still. You don't have to tie them up to get them to stay. They call it ground tying, because you can just leave the rope or reins on the ground and the horse stays put.

Lizzy had never been around a horse like that. She didn't know there was such thing as a horse that ground tied. She simply led Piper out of the barn by the halter rope and then looped the rope over a rail to tie Piper up.

But Piper was having none of it. Because Piper only ground tied. When Lizzy tied her, she felt trapped and her flight instinct kicked in. She panicked as soon as she saw that rope go around the rail, her nostrils flared and her eyes bulged, she reared up and pulled back with every muscle in her mighty back and legs to break free.

Since I wasn't there, I'm not sure of the mechanics involved. But, unfortunately, one of Lizzy's fingers was tangled up in the rope. And as soon as Piper reared and pulled back, it mashed the finger—her left index finger, to be precise—against the rail. The finger stopped moving, but the lead rope, which was attached to Piper, just kept going.

It snapped the finger at the second knuckle, mangling the digit so badly doctors thought they were going to have to take it off.

The only alternative—the only way to save the finger—

was surgery to insert a pin where the knuckle had once flexed, fusing the joint.

Which meant she could no longer do the complex fingerings needed for *Praeludium and Allegro*—or any other piece.

There would be no San Francisco School of Music, no professional violin, no escape from Lodi and the pall of death.

So when Lizzy said her finger hurt, I'm sure it still did.

But it wasn't nearly as bad as the pain of knowing what she had lost.

Chapter

14
Blood

COMING OUT OF LAST CHANCE, a few miles on down the trail, there's a place where two roads meet.

It's nothing special, and if it has an official name, I don't know it. But if a support crew knows what it's doing and where it's going—as Miss Betty certainly did—they can drive to that junction and wait for their riders to come through.

The animals were well-fed and watered by that point. And even though they were starting to lose more water in the soaring heat, it's not strictly necessary for the crews to stop.

This was perhaps the one place where their mission wasn't all about the horses. It was about cheering on the riders and giving them one last reminder—before they get into the depths of the canyons—that they were not alone and that someone out there was pulling for them. By that point in the ride, a lot of the competitors are so saddle-sore and tired, they're happy to have any kind of distraction.

Piper and Jack had been churning along at a good clip since Last Chance, and I think Cowgirl was probably of a mind to not let them break stride as they passed through. In some ways, horses are just like violinists when they get going, they don't want to disrupt a good tempo.

But her plans to simply smile and wave were brought to an end when Doc Jenson put his big body in the middle of the intersection and held up his arms. He wore a stern look on his face.

"What's going on?" Cowgirl asked.

"One of the volunteers was in touch with the National Weather Service," Doc said. "They're trying to put the word out: there's a severe thunderstorm warning for this afternoon. They're telling riders to be careful about being out in the open and reminding them to seek safe shelter if it gets bad."

Miss Betty was appearing from around the side of the van. She had two ponchos, wrapped in plastic.

"You might want to take these," she said, attempting to hand them to Lizzy.

"No thanks," Lizzy said, dabbing her sweat-soaked brow with her T-shirt. "Right now a thunderstorm would be just about perfect."

"Well, now," Miss Betty was starting to say, "why don't you just stick it in Jack's bag and that way you'll—"

"What's going on?" Cowgirl interrupted.

She had ridden up to the van. Being on Piper gave her an easy view into the open side window, where Cowboy was sitting in his chair, looking even more wilted than usual.

"The A/C has been a little on the fritz," Miss Betty said. "He's just a little warm. He'll be—"

"No. That's not it," Cowgirl said. "What's that stain?"

"What are you talking about?"

"The stain. On his pants."

She was looking in the direction of Cowboy's lap. Miss Betty frowned, tucked the unwanted ponchos under her arm, and walked toward the van.

"I must have waited a little too long ," Missy Betty said. "I've been giving him some extra water on account of the heat. I know he doesn't handle it real well, but—"

"But, it's blood," Cowgirl said, her voice cracking.

Cowboy had been passing blood in his urine for some time now. A failing kidney simply can't process all the blood that the body wants it to—especially when there's only one of them—and it soon gets to where it has nowhere else to put it. But Cowboy's output had always been fairly normal, indicating that the kidney was doing at least a little bit of its job.

It had finally stopped altogether. The stain on Cowboy's Wranglers was a deep scarlet.

Miss Betty was opening the side door of the van. "Well, now, I wouldn't say it was—"

She stopped herself. She was now looking at the blood stain with an extra crease on her wrinkled brow. She had been a nurse for long enough. She didn't need anyone to draw her diagrams about what was happening.

"Oh, dear," is all she said. "I'm sorry. I just got so busy with Piper and Jack I hadn't gotten around to changing him and—"

Cowgirl was just staring at the red, transfixed by the vivid color. The visual evidence was so at odds with what she had talked herself into believing.

Cowgirl listened well to what the doctors had told her. She understood her husband was dying and that neither man nor medicine could intercede. She just wasn't ready for it to happen quite so soon.

Whatever duty you would expect a spouse to perform, she had exceeded it. She had dressed him, fed him, treated his bed sores, worried over his infections, bathed him, combed his hair and wiped his weepy eyes every day for eight years. And she had performed all this with, quite literally, without a murmur of thanks from her husband.

Yet there was Cowgirl, still unable or unwilling to let go. Maybe it was because she had come so close to losing him already, she cherished the little bit of him that she had left. As grueling as her daily routine was, the way she acted around him told me she would have kept doing it forever. If only because it would mean she'd still get to be with him.

The shock of being confronted with the knowledge she wouldn't—that the end really was approaching—must have been all over her face. Because when Lizzy rode up, she was reflecting the same fright right back at her mother, in the way that children often are a mirror of their parents' emotions.

And I think seeing her own fright on Lizzy is what made Cowgirl clamp it down. Immediately.

"Momma, what's happening?" Lizzy asked.

"Nothing, baby. Everything is fine."

"Is Daddy okay?"

"Just spilled a little something on his pants. Choppy"—she said the name sharply enough that Choppy, who had been loitering near Doc's truck, looked up immediately—"I've been thinking Jack needs some electrolytes. I don't think he got enough at Robinson Flat. Can you dig some out?"

"*Si si*," he said, walking toward the flat bed and lowering the tailgate.

Doc, who was still standing in the middle of the road, might have raised an eyebrow, because he had personally administered a more-than-adequate dosage of the minerals during the hour hold.

If Cowgirl saw it, she was ignoring it. Instead, she immediately turned to Lizzy. "Well, don't make Choppy walk over here," Cowgirl said. "Go on over there and help."

Lizzy was just confused enough that she did as her mother commanded. She gave Jack a squeeze and steered him toward Doc's truck, which was some twenty yards away from the van—and, more importantly, directly behind it. In a place where Lizzy wouldn't be able to see what Cowgirl was about to do.

She immediately hopped off Piper, who stood still, obediently, just like she had been trained. Miss Betty, who instantly understood what Cowgirl was up to, was already tugging off Cowboy's boots. Cowgirl went for his Wranglers.

"You have a change for him, yes?" Cowgirl asked in a hushed tone, though she didn't even need to say it.

Miss Betty had already gone for a satchel that was off to the side of his wheelchair. Before long, they had him changed into a clean pair of Wranglers.

The last thing Miss Betty did was find a garbage bag and dispose of the carnage: a diaper and a pair of jeans, each blood soaked.

Chapter

15
Tempest

THERE ARE THREE CANYONS that define the middle portion of the Tevis. On a late August afternoon they are like three descents into hell.

As Cowgirl and Lizzy slowly worked their way down into the first one, a kind of gloom had fallen over them.

For Cowgirl, it was what she had just witnessed and the knowledge—hitting her in tsunami-sized waves of understanding—of what it meant. I think there was a part of her that wanted to quit the moment she saw that blood leaking out of her husband. And if it had just been her on that trail, likely she would have.

But she had the other members of her family to think about. Firstly, no matter what the rest of the world thought, Cowgirl firmly believed it was Cowboy's dream to see his wife and daughter finish the Tevis.

Secondly, Cowgirl had this hope and dream of Lizzy winning a belt buckle. She wanted Lizzy to be able to experience that achievement and the pure joy it would bring, without the veil of her father's imminent demise cloaking her eyes.

But there was no clearing that veil from Cowgirl's eyes. So if she was slumped in her saddle as they steadily dropped into the canyon, that was why.

For Lizzy, it was the ride itself that was wearing her down. Each of the sections of the Tevis provides the riders with a different kind of test. The first—up mountains, across boulder fields and over ridges—is a technical challenge. The second, the canyons, is more of a mental and physical grind.

The canyons are traversed by a series of switchbacks that seem to go on forever, with each length of trail taking you perhaps another twenty feet down. That may sound like progress, except when you realize you're trying to get to the bottom of a canyon that's two thousand feet deep.

So you ride for a while, past varmint burrows and boulders, and then do a hairpin turn to the left. Then you ride for a while more, past sage and scrub, and do a hairpin turn right. Then you repeat the thing over and over and over again.

The footing is this loose, gritty rubble, so you can't let your attention wander. Your eyes have to stay locked on the trail, even though all you want to do is close them, to give them even a moment's break from the dust, which is once again chokingly thick.

Since it's downhill and the grade can get fairly severe even the swiftest horses can only go but so fast. Plus, the trail is single track. Cowgirl found herself nose to tail with another horse more often than not, and there were few opportunities to pass.

During the steeper parts, to spare some pounding on their mounts' legs, Cowgirl and Lizzy hopped off and did a combination of running, walking and sliding down the hill. Cowgirl's feet slammed into the pointy toes of her red boots, which weren't really designed with distance running in mind. Lizzy, in her tennis shoes faired better.

Then they would get back in the saddle, just in time to get pelted by small rocks that were kicked loose by riders higher up on the switchbacks and then rained down on those below.

All of this was happening in the hottest part of a sweltering day, under a sun that was as powerful as it was relentless. The forecast predicted by breezeless Cavanaugh Ridge had turned out to be dead—and deadly—accurate. The temperature hit a hundred degrees as they entered the canyon and then kept right on rising, like it had no plan on stopping any time soon.

There's something about those narrow canyons that magnifies the heat. It starts down at the bottom which is always the hottest part because it's the lowest. But then, since hot air rises, it radiates up and hits you in the face.

And this is where the canyon effect really comes in. The walls are so steep, the air can never seem to quite escape out the top. It's just stuck there. The more the sun beats down, the more the effect is amplified.

Ten thousand feet up, where pockets of superheated air from the flatlands to the west were finding the frigid upper atmosphere, thunderclouds were forming. But they were not yet near enough to bring anything resembling relief.

Lizzy and Cowgirl had the additional burden of being blond and fair. They wore brimmed canvas hats. But that meant the heat was that much more trapped around their faces.

It made the trip down toward the bottom of the canyon incredibly trying work. The sweat was streaming out their pores only to mix with the dust that was so omnipresent. Some of it caked on their faces. Some of it rolled into their eyes, the tiny shards slicing at the soft tissue.

All of it brought them misery. Even their braids—Cowgirl's one and Lizzy's two—seemed to droop.

Cowgirl bore the difficulty with typical stoicism. Lizzy allowed herself some early complaining, but eventually lost her enthusiasm for it. Or maybe she realized it wasn't doing any good.

Piper seemed frustrated by a trail that didn't allow her

to run like she wanted to and by not being able to pass other horses.

Jack just kept plodding along in his quiet way.

At the bottom of the first canyon was the North Fork of the Middle Fork of the American River. Cowgirl and Lizzy led Piper and Jack down to the river, where they drank thirstily.

Then they climbed back up the bank and crossed the river on a cable-suspended bridge known as Swinging Bridge. Its name aside, it doesn't really swing *that* much, as long as there aren't too many horses on it at one time. But any more than two or three, and it really does sway quite a bit, enough that it'll spook even the calmest horse—to say nothing of the rider.

Cowgirl went first, keeping the reins a bit tighter in her hand than usual in case Piper got some crazy idea in her head.

Lizzy followed. The bridge isn't that high over the river, but it is narrow, with handrails that are well below where the saddle sits on a big mule like Jack. Lizzy kept her eyes closed the whole way.

They were now at the bottom of the canyon, the reward for which being that they had the honor of climbing back up the other side, rising on the same kind of interminable switchbacks that got them down there.

It was every bit as dusty and grinding. The only difference being it was a bit hotter now.

After perhaps ten switchbacks, as they passed within a few feet of each other on one of the hairpin turns, Lizzy let out a loud, "Mom, this sucks."

Cowgirl, who had been chewing on an unlit blue tip match, shifted the mashed wood from one side of her mouth to the other. "Yep," she said.

And they continued on up.

For Cowgirl and Lizzy, time seemed to have stopped. Climbing that canyon was one of those experiences that, when you're in the middle of it, you swear you can't even remember your life before you got into the canyon; and you're quite sure you'll never get out. It was just one switchback after another.

"Keep drinking," Cowgirl called out at one point, not bothering to turn around.

When she didn't hear a reply, she said, "Did you hear me? I said keep drinking."

Then she turned to see Lizzy had a water bottle tipped to her lips. She hadn't needed her mother's reminder.

They didn't give much thought to the clouds that were beginning to pile up in the distance. They just kept climbing as the sun pounded, the dust choked, and the stifling air seemed to run out of oxygen.

As they neared the top of the canyon rim, the largest and puffiest of the gathering, cumulonimbus clouds had finally mustered enough height that they blocked the sun. A breeze was suddenly stirring.

As the shade prevailed over them, Cowgirl looked up, a mix of relief and concern on her face. As if to justify her growing fear, the first peel of thunder rumbled in the distance.

"Whoo-hoo!" Lizzy called out from behind. "Thank God! I hope we get soaked."

Cowgirl didn't say anything. In the Sierra Nevada, thunderstorms can come up with astonishing speed, and, from the way the wind was suddenly strengthening, this one seemed to be approaching fast.

Too fast. Cowgirl's eyes were cast toward the top of the ridge, a treeless slab of granite that would leave them totally exposed should the storm hit while they were crossing it.

On the other side was the cover of a thick stand of lodgepole pines. The question was whether they'd get there in time.

Cowgirl was trying to calculate the answer as she studied the storm, then looked back at the trail, then up at the clouds again. The problem was, because of all the riders behind them, they couldn't stop without creating a backup. And yet, because of all the riders ahead, they couldn't make a break for it either.

They were stuck with whatever fate their inalterable speed and the unswerving storm left them with.

The sky grew darker, gloomier. The worst of it seemed to be looming over them all of a sudden. The sun that had been so scorching mere minutes earlier was now completely blotted out by a lead-colored cloud.

The first drops of rain were fat and hot, and they began hitting Cowgirl and Lizzy when they were perhaps a half a mile from the top. Another growl of thunder sounded. A gust of wind kicked up, nearly knocking off Cowgirl's hat.

Cowgirl clamped it down tighter on her head. Lizzy let out another whoop, so thrilled was she by this development. Cowgirl just peered up anxiously. Then she saw a wall of rain powering toward them, driven by the wind and swooping down from above.

They were about a quarter of a mile from the top of the ridge when it reached them, sending water tumbling down on their heads in terrific sheets. A crack of lightning sounded, followed almost immediately by a boom of thunder. The rain and wind roared. The tempest was right on top of them, and it was announcing itself in full throat. Creation itself was not as noisy as a summer thunderstorm in the Sierra Nevada.

Visibility had gone from miles to feet in a matter of minutes. Jack and Piper kept putting one foot in front of another, now working their way across the granite slab, which had become slick from rain. Cowgirl and Lizzy weren't even sure if they were on the trail, adding to the general sense of confusion.

The wind-driven water was coming down so hard it scoured their skin. Lizzy, who had suddenly lost her fervor for a good drenching, had her head bowed and tilted to the side, in an attempt to shield her face from the worst of it. Her faded green chaps had become dark with moisture.

Cowgirl, still in the lead, let the blue tip match drop from her mouth as she urged Piper forward. The rain mixed with the sweat that had slickened the muscles on her arms and made them shine, like they had been oiled. It ran down her shirt and into her pants and boots until there was no more dry to be wet.

The air had an ionized ozone smell so thick they could taste it. This sickly sweet wrapped around their tongues. The animals could feel the charge tingling through their metal shoes and up their legs. They were getting close to the top. Their forest sanctuary loomed somewhere in the distance, even though they could no longer see it.

The rain seemed to pause for just a moment, almost like the storm was gathering itself. Then, no more than forty feet in front of them, a lightning bolt struck.

It was like a jagged edge of light spearing up or striking down or some combination of both. It was so powerful it seemed to shake the air. The clap of thunder that came with it had its own concussion, one they could feel in their chests.

Piper reared high and veered mindlessly to the left, her eyes bulging with terror. Cowgirl pulled hard on the right rein, trying to stop the spin, but the Arab reared again. Acting on an instinct born during thousands of hours in the saddle, Cowgirl stood in the stirrups, leaned far forward and pushed the reins down hard to lower Piper's head and keep the horse from flipping over backwards. It saved them from a nasty tumble down to the hard granite below. But it did nothing to settle Piper.

The horse came down and spun some more, her titanium shoes scraping and slipping on the wet stone slab. Cowgirl was calmly saying, "Whoa, girl, whoa," but it could barely be heard over the reverberations of the thunder, the roar of the rain, and Piper's own terrified whinnies.

Piper couldn't be calmed. She was so crazed she seemed almost determined to hurt someone, either herself or Cowgirl. Or both.

When a horse gets like that, there's nothing a rider can do but hang on. The horse is well beyond having sense talked into it, and it won't respond to the reins. Piper reared back again and let out another cry.

Lizzy was momentarily paralyzed, too terrified by the whole scene—both the lightning strike and Piper's frenzy—to be able to do much about it.

It was Jack, so prepossessed was he toward tranquility, who got it in his mind that if no one else could do anything, he'd just have to solve this predicament himself. He took a few steps toward Piper, not so close that he was in danger of getting kicked, but close enough that he could fill Piper's frame of vision with his steady presence.

Once Piper got that simple reminder that Jack was still there, by her side like always, she stopped rearing. Her eyes no longer bulged. She turned in one more circle, but Jack took a few steps closer so she couldn't keep spinning without bumping into him.

This ended with Jack standing shoulder to shoulder, flank to flank with Piper, so close that Cowgirl's and Lizzy's knees were touching. The effect was more powerful than any sedative Doc Jenson could have shot into the horse. Piper, who moments before seemed determined to tear herself to pieces, was now still.

Lizzy was biting her upper lip, the shock of it all not yet worn off. Cowgirl was trying to bring her breathing back under control, knowing that Piper could feel it if her rider was distressed.

But once Cowgirl had taken a few deep inhales and

followed it with a few controlled exhales, she reached out and patted the mule.

"Good boy, Jack," she said. "Good boy."

She breathed deeply again. Then another rumble of thunder sounded in the far distance. Cowgirl gave Piper a squeeze, and they hustled toward the safety of the forest haven, with Jack dutifully bringing up the rear.

Chapter

16

Hee-haw

ONE WOULD THINK THIS HARROWING ORDEAL raised the riders' spirits, allowing them to feel like they had won an important victory over the worst the Tevis could throw at them, fortify them for what lay ahead.

But, if anything, it seemed the opposite was true. Cowgirl was still a bit rattled by how close they had come to calamity, either from the lightning strike or the terror it provoked in her horse. This, in turn, led to feelings of self-doubt, like maybe a Tevis buckle was just not something she was meant to win.

She had trained herself to stamp out such negative thoughts, having developed immense wells of discipline over years of trial. But the only way to call on them was to withdraw further into herself.

Which just looked like sulking to her riding companion, who was now even more demoralized than before. Lizzy had never seen her mother sulk.

Lizzy was becoming more convinced it was folly for her to have started the Tevis in the first place. And any thought she had of reaching out to her mother for encouragement was thwarted by the belief that Cowgirl was brooding.

Physically, they were more uncomfortable than ever.

They were soaked. All that wetness had settled in to every crevice of their beings, such that their clothing and skin chafed against one another everywhere they came into contact.

On top of that, the sun returned with a terrible vengeance as soon as the storm passed, as if it was determined to make up for the momentary respite from the heat its absence had provided. There were still fat drops of water falling from the trees, hitting their hats and shoulders with loud plunks. And there was now steam rising up from below, making the whole mix that much more sultry.

As if that wasn't enough, a swarm of mosquitoes, reveling in the superheated humidity, had materialized to attack the riders' exposed skin and feast on their blood

So in addition to being sullen, wet, dirty, hot and irritated, they were now bug-ravaged as well.

But, the Tevis, being the cruel taskmaster it often is, there was more difficulty ahead. Coming out of Swinging Bridge Canyon, after that brief jaunt through that buggy forest, there comes another ascent, up to a geological formation known as Devil's Thumb.

The thumb part of the name is pretty obvious. It was created a long time ago by an hydraulic mining operation that washed away all the loose dirt and stone but left behind a forty-foot-tall monlith that really does resemble a thumb.

The devil part is just because of everything else about it.

For the riders, who are roughly ten hours into their journey by this point, it's a kind of psychological warfare, another grinding climb to follow the grinding climb they just completed. For the horses, it can be like the marathoner's equivalent of "the wall", that obstacle that just knocks their will clean out of them. And, being that horse and rider are so intimately connected, each is feeling the other's pain.

It was just more slow, difficult work, being performed at roughly 3 o'clock in the afternoon, as the temperature had resumed its climb back above a hundred degrees and beyond. Cowgirl and Lizzy were alone by this point, the storm having separated and scattered the pack. They did not speak as their mounts plodded upward. Their suffering did not require conversation to confirm its existence.

There was a water stop at Devil's Thumb, which the equines badly needed by that point. Piper and Jack did not require encouragement. Cowgirl and Lizzy had barely dismounted before the animals plunged their heads into the water troughs and began sucking deeply in an attempt to replace some of the fluid they had lost.

Cowgirl went to her pack on Piper's saddle and pulled out a granola bar. Lizzy found the shade of a tarp that had been erected by one of the volunteers and had flopped under it, trying to rub the ache out of her legs as she lay there.

Other riders straggled up to Devil's Thumb looking every bit as haggard as Cowgirl and Lizzy. One of them, a gray-haired man with a shaggy beard that was not suited to such conditions, walked his horse over to one of the water tubs. Moments after his horse put its muzzle in the tub to drink, the man dunked his whole head in. The horse was so thirsty, it didn't even stir.

Cowgirl stayed on her feet, keeping the blood moving in her legs, as Piper and Jack had their fill. If she had gazed along a straight line to the northeast, the direction they had come from, she would have gotten the satisfaction of knowing everything she and her daughter had traveled over every bit of countryside she could see.

I don't think she would have wanted to look to the southwest. Because they had all that and more to go.

When the animals were done drinking they were led by the reins over to welcomed shade. Lizzy was splayed on the ground.

"Okay," Cowgirl said. "It's time."

Lizzy looked up at her mother with some mix of defiance, loathing, and exhaustion. But mostly exhaustion.

"Nope," she said. "I really am done now."

Cowgirl did not reply.

"There's no way I'm getting back in that saddle," Lizzy said, as if trying to head off any argument before it could even start. "I just...I can't anymore. I did half a Tevis. That's going to have to be good enough."

Cowgirl's jaw muscles flexed as her molars ground into one another.

"One of the volunteers told me it's not far to the gate-and-go at Deadwood," Lizzy continued. "It's a nice logging road, a little bit downhill. Jack and I are going to walk there and then they have trailers for all the horses that get disqualified there. They'll take us to Michigan Bluff, where I can meet up with the team."

Cowgirl nodded her head. "I see," she said, letting out a long sigh. "So you've made up your mind?"

"Yeah, Mom. I'm done."

"Are you sure?"

Lizzy nodded her head. "I'm sorry, Mom."

Cowgirl looked down at the ground. "Well, then I guess we're done, too."

Lizzy immediately sat up. "What? No. Just Jack and me. You and Piper are going to go and get you a buckle. She's in great shape."

Cowgirl shook her head. "It doesn't work that way. We're a team. If we can't finish together, we quit together. That's how it goes."

"No," Lizzy said. "No, no, no. That's not...The Tevis is your thing, Mom. You talk about it all year long. You see horses in your dreams. I don't. I'm just...You can't quit because I wasn't ready for it. You can't do that to me."

Cowgirl raised one eyebrow. "Excuse me? What am *I* doing to *you* here?"

"You can't make me the bad guy like that. That's not fair."

"Not fair?" her mother asked.

"Yeah. Just...*go*. I'll be fine."

"Maybe *you'll* be fine, but *we* won't be. You know Piper seldom goes anywhere without Jack. Did you see that horse during the storm? We've got forty-something miles left to go. She'll never make it without Jack. She'll spook at her own shadow the moment he's out of her sight."

"Then take Jack. He's gone without a rider a million times. I'll walk by myself."

Cowgirl was shaking her head. "Nope. It's one equine, one rider. Those are Tevis rules. If I have two mounts, I'll be disqualified. Now, I'm going to tell the head volunteer to radio ahead that one-eighty-eight and one-eight-nine are packing it in. I can't have them waiting for us, expecting us to come through the vet check."

"No, Mom—"

Cowgirl started walking, a set of reins in each hand. Lizzy was on her feet now, a sudden rush of energy making her forget the ache in her legs.

"Mom, stop. Don't do that. Just go on without me."

Cowgirl didn't turn back to acknowledge her daughter. She was walking, head held as high as ever, in the direction of a volunteer with a handheld radio.

"I just hate it when you do this to me." Lizzy screamed.

This made Cowgirl's head snap back. Maybe there are fourteen-year-olds who serve up that kind of phrase to their mothers on a regular basis, but Lizzy had never uttered such before. And Cowgirl was too stunned to immediately respond.

"Why do we always have to do everything your way?" Lizzy continued. "Why is it we always have to do everything exactly your way?"

Lizzy was now charging toward her mother and yelling. "This isn't even my dream. This was never my dream. *This* was my dream."

She was waving her splinted hand in the air. "But I guess

that doesn't even matter anymore."

Cowgirl had stopped walking. Lizzy stormed up to her and ripped the reins out of her hand.

But not Jack's reins. Piper's reins. In one swift movement that belied the fatigue she had been complaining of mere moments earlier, Lizzy vaulted herself into the Arab's saddle.

Then she flared her legs out wide and, with all the force she could muster, buried her heels in Piper's rib cage.

For a horse with Piper's unfailingly kind eye, a horse that had grown accustomed to only the gentlest treatment after a year of Cowgirl's schooling, this was a rude kind of shock. This was a return to the days of Duke Dawson, he of the heavy hand and jagged spurs, and Piper responded with a start.

She burst forward down that wide logging road like another lightning bolt was going to bury itself in her flank if she didn't move out, doing her best impersonation of a Thoroughbred springing from the start gate at the Kentucky Derby. She was soon flying down that logging trail at a gallop, full of spite and determination, with Lizzy clinging tightly to her.

Cowgirl swore and legged up on Jack, who didn't need much encouragement to give chase.

The only thing was, Piper had more speed in her legs than Jack. In a sprint like that, a mule just isn't a match for an Arab. And Piper, who already had a head start, was only adding to the distance between her and Jack. First a hundred yards. Then two hundred.

Realizing she was never going to catch them—and not wanting to burn out the mule, especially so close to a vet check—Cowgirl finally eased off. She returned Jack slowly to a canter, then a trot.

Lizzy raced on, kicking up a small cloud of dust. She

was soon small in the distance, then disappeared around a bend.

Jack just watched, his candlestick ears pricked forward, like he was trying to make out the last sounds of Piper's ever-more-distant footsteps. He tried surging forward, to go after her, but Cowgirl held him back.

"Whoa, boy," Cowgirl said. "Let 'em go."

And then she added: "Sometimes, that's just what you have to do."

Jack came to a stop, but his body was unusually ill-at-ease. His wet nose wriggled. His brown neck twitched to the right. Something was happening deep within the animal, way down in his gut somewhere.

He flattened his head just slightly, took in a huge breath and opened his mouth wide, baring his enormous teeth and extending his brilliant-red tongue.

And then, for the first time in all the years Cowgirl had known him—for the first time in his life, as far as anyone knew—he let out a cacophonous "hee." Then he exhaled more and out burst a "haw," a real mule hee-haw, high to low, piercing and ear-splitting.

Then another. Then another. They just kept busting out.

It was as if he had been constructing them in his cavernous head, just waiting for the right time to let them escape. And now, here, in the moment he deemed properly dire, more than fifty miles into this epic journey, they emerged with a sound as big as the Sierra Nevada themselves. They tumbled down the trail, rose on the afternoon thermals, and echoed off the faces of the nearby mountains.

I couldn't say how long it took for the sound to reach Piper's ears. Nor do I know how long the Arab needed to properly interpret the message. Nor could I even guess the exact content of the message. Was he calling out to his friend, Piper? Or was he calling to Lizzy, telling her to come back? Since I don't speak mule, I couldn't even offer a guess.

But some short amount of time after the last of those hee-haws went booming out of Jack, there came an answer. It was not nearly as loud. But it was discernible nevertheless.

This high and urgent whinny.

Not waiting for Cowgirl to squeeze her legs on his sides, Jack tore off, hee-hawing as he ran, his hooves churning up clods of dirt. When he heard another whinny, he accelerated. Cowgirl simply hung on.

When they reached the corner that Piper had so recently disappeared around, they saw her standing there. Riderless.

Lizzy was on her feet, already walking back up the trail. Jack slowed as he saw her, then came to a stop as soon as she was close enough to reach out for him.

"Jack, boy, I heard you boy! I heard you!" she said. There were tears coming from her eyes.

"I didn't know you had it in you, boy!" She kissed his forehead, pet his ears, then put her cheek next to his frothing muzzle.

"I'm sorry for leaving you, boy. I'm sorry. I won't do it again. I promise."

Having made his point, Jack was back to his mute self. Piper stamped her feet and snorted.

Then Lizzy looked up at Cowgirl. Each held the glance for a long moment.

What was communicated between them was, to a cowboy like me, every bit as impenetrable as what the mule had said. An apology? A pardon? A peace-offering? I don't speak teenager, either. Or mother. Especially when neither of them is actually talking.

But some kind of understanding must have passed between them. Because, eventually, Lizzy said, "Let's just go."

To which Cowgirl said, "Yep."

Chapter

17

El Dorado Canyon

THEY SWITCHED BACK to their original mounts before arriving at Deadwood, with Cowgirl leading them at a gentle trot the rest of the way.

Even still, they were entering the gate-and-go too hot. Probably in more ways than one, but certainly when it came to the animals. There was no way they could pass the pulse check right away as they had at the previous stops.

Cowgirl swung off Piper, found a sponge, and rubbed the horse down. Lizzy did the same with Jack.

They still weren't really talking. The parts that had just been rubbing against each other were too raw.

As they waited for Piper's and Jack's hearts to slow, they gazed around the clearing. On one side, there were half-a-dozen horses waiting to be loaded into a large trailer.

The looks on the nearby humans' faces said it all. These were the horses that didn't make it.

"They're dropping like flies," Lizzy said quietly.

"It's so hot," Cowgirl said. "Hottest Tevis I've ever known."

"Think we're going to make it?"

That Lizzy was using the plural pronoun was a good sign. So was the renewed bounce to her stride. But it was still too fragile for Cowgirl to remark on it, lest she disrupt it from developing into something more durable.

"We just have to be smart," Cowgirl said.

"'Wisely, and slow. They stumble that run fast.' Isn't that right?"

Lizzy was smiling awkwardly. This was definitely a peace offering. Maybe not for a full and lasting armistice. But certainly for a temporary ceasefire.

"Something like that, yes," Cowgirl said, returning the smile.

Lizzy went back to her work. Cowgirl did the same, stealing glances at her daughter as she did so, trying to gauge just where the girl's head was. It used to be she almost always knew. Not anymore.

It wasn't only the spewed anger that had shocked Cowgirl. It was what came after. Cowgirl never realized that Lizzy resented her for the accident that mangled her finger. And she didn't know how to even approach the topic without ripping open more than just Lizzy's surgical sutures.

So they continued the rubdown in silence. As they finished up, they were approached by a volunteer, a man with a handheld radio, thick glasses and a frown.

"Afternoon," he said. "How's your ride going?"

"We're here," Cowgirl said.

"I guess you are," he said, then adjusted his glasses. "Well, just wanted to let you know we're getting some reports from up ahead on the trail...I suppose you're aware there were some lightning strikes in the area?"

"Well aware," Cowgirl said, and left it at that.

"It looks like one of them has touched off a brush fire that seems to be growing pretty fast. It's southeast of Auburn, somewhere. We don't know yet if it's threatening the trail. The Forest Service Rangers are tracking it. They're aware we're out here, of course. But they say their first concern is protecting the town, not the trail. They're just trying to keep it on the east side of the river. So if the fire wants to go toward the trail, they're going to let it."

"Got it," Cowgirl said.

"It's nothing to be too worried about yet. But we're letting people know. Maybe another thunderstorm will come through and put it out for us."

"Yep," Cowgirl said.

The man with the glasses nodded, then moved on.

Cowgirl nodded toward Piper and Jack. "Think they're ready for the vet check?"

"I don't know, Mom. They were going pretty fast."

"Your call," Cowgirl said. This was *her* peace offering.

Lizzy held her hand to Jack's neck. She needed longer than Cowgirl. She actually had to do the math. "Yeah, I guess so," she said.

"All right, let's do it then."

With Lizzy in the lead, they found a free veterinarian, a woman who had tied her big shock of busy, red hair back to keep it off her neck.

"Number one-eighty-eight and one-eight-nine," Lizzy said.

"Okay," the vet replied.

Cowgirl and Lizzy gave the woman their cards. She already had her stopwatch out and her hand on Jack's neck. The vet had a discouraged look on her face like she had been delivering too much bad news to too many riders.

But then the face changed.

"Sixty," she said. "Good for you."

She moved on to Piper, counting silently. "And fifty-six for this girl. Good work, you two. Or should I say you four."

There was now a smile on her lips. "I have to tell you, I haven't seen any animals looking as good as these two in quite some time. I'm going to keep this in mind when it comes time to vote for the Haggin."

"Thank you," Cowgirl said. "We do appreciate."

The vet dipped her head up and back. "You've heard about the forest fire?"

"Yep," Cowgirl said.

"All right. Be careful out there. Stay cool."

But that, of course, was pretty much impossible given what was coming next.

El Dorado Canyon is the largest and deepest of the three major chasms that slice through the Western States Trail. It borrows its name from Spanish explorers, who believed there was a city made of gold somewhere in South America, if only they knew where to look for it.

The 49ers coming to California in the mid-19th century thought this canyon, which had gold deposits lying exposed on the creek bed when they first found it, was their El Dorado.

There's no gold there anymore. Just a whole lot of sage brush, chaparral, loose rock, and hard work. And Cowgirl and Lizzy were hitting it during the peak of the afternoon heat.

They repeated the same procedure as they had through the first canyon, switchback by unending switchback. On some of the steeper parts, they hopped off their saddles and walked.

At one point, they passed within ten feet of a rattlesnake baking itself on a rock. The snake gave its tail an ominous shake, sending that chilling, bone dry sound out into the air.

Cowgirl and Lizzy both spun their heads in the direction of the serpent. The equines didn't. They were so focused on the trail, their necks stayed straight, pointing them ever downward.

It was roughly four o'clock when they neared El Dorado Creek at the bottom of the canyon.

As they drew close, they heard a curious sound down near the creek. It was an old man, whooping and hollering every time a rider came through. His cheering echoed well up the canyon wall, but he wasn't just offering encouragement. He was also reading off the temperature, then giving his own editorial comments on the matter.

"Hundred and twelve in the shade," he cackled as someone got close. "A Tevis record!"

"Hundred and twelve. They say it's one-oh-eight in Sacramento today, so that's where you go if you want to cool off!"

Cowgirl and Lizzy didn't know whether they should laugh or groan. The old timer kept up his commentary, offering something different to each rider who came through without repeating himself.

Cowgirl and Lizzy finally saw him. He had disheveled white hair and tattered clothes, making him look like the ghost of an old 49er. He had a small flask of something that may or may or not have been water, and he was tilting it back toward his lips until he saw them.

"The mother and daughter Tevis team!" he yelled, lowering the flask. "They said you'd be coming through. Everyone's been talking about you!"

Cowgirl tipped her hat in his direction. Lizzy just grinned. They hopped out of their saddles, allowing Piper and Jack to go toward the creek.

The old man's donkey, which he had apparently led down into the canyon from whatever hole he crawled out of, was grazing on a small patch of grass that grew alongside the creek. A cart that looked as old as its owner, with one wheel that had gone slightly askew, was parked nearby. It contained food, water and camping gear, because apparently the old man decided to make an expedition of it.

As Piper and Jack sucked water, the old man consulted the thermometer he had hanging from the branch of the cottonwood he was standing under.

"Hundred and twelve...call it hundred twelve and a half

for the mother-daughter team. A new record! You know just downstream from here is an old mining camp they used to call 'Baked Oven.' Bet they named it on a day like this."

Cowgirl smiled again and took a long swig from her water bottle. Lizzy was a few yards away on her knees next to the creek, just upstream from the animals, splashing water on her face and head. Her hair, which had taken on red highlights from all the dust, was slowly working its way back to blond.

Once Lizzy was done with her miner's bath and Jack and Piper had drunk all they could, Cowgirl and Lizzy saddled back up. As they crossed the creek, the old man was already calling out to the next group of riders.

They were most of the way up the other side of the canyon when they came across another unusual sight, this one more ominous than a drunken weatherman.

It was a middle aged woman, a Tevis rider, except she was out of her saddle and slumped against a boulder next to the trail. She was slender, with light brown hair and dazed expression. Her skin had blushing scarlet undertones.

Her horse was a big, bay-colored fellow who was just standing in the middle of the trail. She was muttering to herself softly.

Cowgirl brought Piper to a stop. Jack halted behind them.

"Are you okay there?" Cowgirl asked.

"Split pea soup," the woman said.

"Ma'am, are you okay?"

"I love split pea soup," the woman said.

Cowgirl slid off and approached her. The woman looked up blankly, without comprehension. For as scorching as it was, the woman was no longer sweating, an ominous sign.

There's a concept in emergency medicine known as

"the golden hour." It's the notion that when a body has been dealt a critical blow, such as a heatstroke, you have about an hour to do something about it before the damage becomes irreversible. It's the hour in which organs can begin to shut down and all kinds of terrible things begin happening inside. The final result—be it death or recovery—might not come for days or even weeks. But actions taken during that golden hour can determine the outcome.

"What's your name, ma'am?" Cowgirl asked.

Cowgirl put her hand on the woman's arm. The woman looked positively bewildered by this intrusion into her world, like she hadn't noticed Cowgirl ride up and was now startled to see another human being kneeling by her side.

"What's your name, Ma'am?" Cowgirl repeated.

"Clementine," she finally said, "Clemmy."

"Clemmy, what's your last name?"

Clementine just stared at Cowgirl.

"What's your horse's name?" Cowgirl asked.

This, at least, she knew: "Chancellor."

"Clemmy, have you been drinking enough water?"

Every Tevis rider knows to drink before they're thirsty. But sometimes, when those canyon ovens really get cooking, a body can't keep enough of the water its owner is putting into it.

Clemmy was just looking down at her arm again, still perplexed. Cowgirl stood and looked at Lizzy.

"Stay with her," Cowgirl said. "Don't let her wander off. If you can get some water in her, great. If not, just take whatever water you have left and dump it on her head. You understand?"

Lizzy, who didn't need a lecture on the dangers of being severely dehydrated when it was 112.5 degrees outside, just said, "Got it."

"I'm going for help," Cowgirl said, then again added, "Just stay here."

Cowgirl swung up on Piper.

Then she leaned forward in the saddle and put her gentle hands on either side of Piper's braided mane. And, in the softest voice, almost a murmur from her heart, Cowgirl whispered, "Jack doesn't need any extra miles on him about now. We're gonna leave him behind, but just for a bit. Then we'll be right back".

Who knows what Piper comprehended. Quite possibly she just sensed the general urgency of the moment. Or maybe she had more assurance after her solo sprint with Lizzy back at Devil's Thumb. Or maybe she still had the comfort of Jack's hee-haw serenade filling her massive heart. Whatever it was, she seemed to translate Cowgirl's message and be quite up for her ask.

It was a mile to Michigan Bluff, and the golden hour clock was ticking. Cowgirl collected the reins and gave Piper a subtle squeeze and a soft "Go."

With no hesitation, Piper shot off leaving a cloud of dust in her wake.

Chapter

18

Truth

BACK IN THE MIDDLE OF THE 19TH CENTURY, Michigan Bluff, California was such a bustling place that it nearly became a victim of its own success. Between the blasting, washing, sluicing and lumbering of the surrounding land, the natural process of erosion was expedited by a few eons and the landslides became so bad the townsfolk had to pack up everything and move. The town was literally going downhill.

Nothing nearly that dramatic happens there anymore. On most any other mid-summer day—most any other day, period—Michigan Bluff is now a sleepy mountain town nestled among huge stands of pine trees. There's no such thing as a traffic jam because there's no such thing as traffic on the narrow road that passes through it.

The one noted exception is the day of the Tevis when Michigan Bluff is the sight of the vet check that marks the two-thirds point of the race. Then it becomes overrun by trucks, trailers, and the fevered efforts of the support teams to give their riders one final push toward the finish line.

There had been talk of moving the vet check elsewhere because Michigan Bluff was getting so congested. For now, Doc and Choppy were one in a line of pickups, waiting to get in the staging area. They were sitting in Doc's F-350, the

A/C blasting as high as it could go but still not taking all the sweat off them. They hadn't spoken much since they had last parted with Cowgirl and Lizzy at that nameless intersection many miles earlier.

They were creeping forward one car-length at a time, Doc's big right foot spending a lot more time on the brake than on the gas. The only noise, other than the rush of the cool-ish air, was Glen Campbell on the radio, telling the world he was a "rhinestone cowboy".

It was Choppy who broke the silence.

"The mule back there, he didn't need electrolytes," he said.

"What are you talking about?" Doc asked, even though he probably knew.

"At that pull off before. Cowgirl told me to get some electrolytes for Jack. You gave him plenty at Robinson Flat."

"So? It's hot as hell out here. I'm sure she was just being cautious. Better too many than too few."

"I think something was wrong with my *hombre*," Choppy said. "And I think Cowgirl didn't want Lizzy to see it."

"Something's been wrong with your *hombre* for eight years now."

"You know what I mean."

Doc didn't respond. Choppy pressed the issue: "What's going on? Did you see something back there? Come on. You have to know. You're a doctor."

"A veterinarian."

"A man's not that different from a horse."

Doc's mouth twitched.

"Come on, Doc. How bad is it? I'm his friend. His *hombre*. You can tell me...how long has he got, you think?"

Doc had been driving with his left hand. The question prompted him to put his right hand up on the steering wheel.

"I don't...I don't have a lot of experience with this sort of thing. It's awful to say, but if he were a horse he wouldn't be having this problem, because we would have put him down a long time ago."

When Choppy didn't reply, Doc added, "We're more humane to animals than we are to ourselves most of the time."

Choppy turned away, peering out the passenger side window as they rolled another few feet then again came to a stop.

"You think it'll happen today?" Choppy asked.

"Tough to say. It's pretty obvious there's a lot of poison building up in his body right now. That kidney of his is finally giving up. You can see it in his color. All I can tell you…when his time is up, he'll just quietly slip out the exit gate."

"I just want to know when to say goodbye."

"You might want to do it real soon then," Doc said.

They continued on without conversation as they neared the parking area. Dolly Parton was now on the radio, working nine to five.

Again, it was Choppy who spoke.

"You think he knows? You think he knows what's happening?"

"Don't ask me that," Doc said.

"Come on. It's just us here. No Cowgirl. No Miss Betty. *Dios mio*, I know what they think. And I know they have to think that way. But...man, I just don't know. I knew him before, you know? I knew what he was like, and..."

Choppy's voice trailed off.

"So you don't think he has any idea what's going on?" Doc asked.

"Maybe that's just what I hope."

Doc shifted his body in his seat. They were almost to the parking spot a volunteer was guiding them toward.

"Now, come on," Choppy pressed. "What do you think?"

"I think I'm not qualified to offer an opinion either way,"

Doc said. "But I will say that man seems to have a fearsome will to live. He's been defying his body for a long time just to make it this far. There's gotta be something he's been wanting to stick around for. Maybe it's this."

"So he knows?"

"Yeah," Doc said. "Deep down, I think he does."

Once Miss Betty pulled in next to them a few minutes later, Doc and Choppy began setting up their team station just as they had at Robinson Flat.

Doc was up ahead putting together the tarp. Miss Betty was helping him, leaving the van running and the air conditioning sputtering away for Cowboy's benefit.

Choppy was going back and forth, bringing more feed and hay and sweating.

As he returned for perhaps his sixth trip, he was approached by the pair of ranch hands who smelled as if they decided the best way to beat a hot day was to bathe themselves in malted beverage. One wore a straw hat. The other wore a baseball cap from a feed store.

"Hey, big man, how you doin' down there?" Straw Hat said, mock toasting him with a can of Bud.

Choppy was, unfortunately, no stranger to this kind of stupidity. He encountered some form of it—usually a lot more subtle than this—every day of his life.

As a younger man, when he was a little more full of spit and vinegar, he'd challenge a bully like this to a fight. Most of them backed down. Those who didn't quickly learned an important lesson about just how much a dislocated kneecap could hurt.

Now that he was a little older and out of his brawling days, Choppy ignored bullies like these, having decided they weren't worth his time or energy. And so he continued toward the flatbed of Doc's truck, like he hadn't heard a word.

"Yo! Stretch! What's going on?" Feed Store said, then took a pull on his beer.

"Maybe he don't *habla Englais*," Straw Hat replied.

"Maybe he only hablas it *un poco*. Makin' his language like the rest of him."

Feed Store laughed at his own invention, which he considered among the finer pieces of wordplay he had ever constructed.

"Hey, *amigo*. *Que pasa*?" Straw Hat said, blocking Choppy's path.

This gave Choppy no choice but to confront the man.

"I'm fine," he said. "And I'm not your *amigo*. So move out of my way. I have work to do."

"What?" Feed Store said. "Like gettin' some hay? I got your hay right here."

Feed Store balanced his beer on the side of Doc's flat bed, grabbed a flake of hay and held it above Choppy's head. "Come on. Just reach up and get it. Jump for it. Jump. You can do it."

As Straw Hat howled, Feed Store kept putting it lower and lower until it was practically on top of Choppy's head. Then Feed Store tossed it to his buddy, who caught it awkwardly, then put his beer down so he could get a better grip.

Choppy didn't budge.

"What, you don't want to play keep away?" Feed Store said. "It's a new game. Instead of monkey in the middle, it's half-pint in the middle."

Choppy stood with his arms crossed, eyeing the man's kneecaps. It had been a few years, but he hadn't forgotten his signature move. All it would take was one swift kick to the side of the bone and Feed Store would never again utter that phrase without the memory of a searing pain shooting up his leg.

"Whatsamatter," Straw Hat said, taunting Choppy with

the hay, like he was going to throw it at him. "You don't want to play with us?"

Feed Store, who was now off to the side having retrieved his beer, laughed and said, "Nah, he's tired out from chasing his best friend's wife."

Choppy couldn't help himself. His head jerked toward Feed Store, who finally knew he'd landed a verbal punch.

"Aww, look at that," Feed Store said. "He's all tuckered out."

Choppy returned his gaze to the kneecaps in front of him. Straw Hat was still faking like he was going to toss the hay.

"You want it?" Straw Hat said. "You want it?"

Choppy lifted his foot just to get a sense for the weight of his boot—and gauge how quickly he could get it flying in the direction of his target.

Then he put his foot back down.

"Keep it," Choppy said, elbowing past Straw Hat and climbing up into the flat bed where he got his own leaf of hay.

Having failed to get a rise out of Choppy, Straw Hat tossed the hay back in the flat bed.

"Aw, come on, man," Straw Hat said. "We're just having some fun with you."

Choppy fixed him with an unswerving gaze.

"You," he said, "are nothing but *'tontos'*. "Fools".

And then he walked away.

Chapter

19

Michigan Bluff

PIPER WILLINGLY CANTERED THE MILE to Michigan Bluff in less than four minutes and Cowgirl didn't slow her down until she spied a volunteer with a two-way radio.

"We got a rider down about a mile back," she said. "Looks like she's got heatstroke. She's in a bad way. We need an ambulance."

The man turned toward her languidly, the heat of the afternoon slowing his movement.

"Ambulance," Cowgirl said. "Ambulance. Now."

The words finally got through to the man. He brought the radio to his mouth and began talking. He listened for a bit, talked some more, then turned to Cowgirl.

"Nearest ambulance is at Foresthill. It's fifteen minutes away at best."

Cowgirl uttered a rare curse. "Okay. Well, tell them to hustle."

She started looking around for a water source so she could at least refill her canteen—and maybe a few others she could borrow—and speed back to Clemmy and Lizzy.

Then a much better idea came to her, mostly because she heard a voice faintly calling out, "Buck a bag! Get your ice, buck a bag!"

Cowgirl pointed Piper toward the sound and was soon riding up to the Good Humor truck.

"Iceberg!" she said sharply.

The amiable Iceberg flashed her a big smile. But his straight white teeth soon vanished as Cowgirl explained the urgency of the situation. It took them exactly five minutes to load Piper's flanks with four twenty-pound bags of ice, two on each side, all secured with the burlap and bailing twine Iceberg had squirrelled away in his truck.

Piper pretty clearly wasn't enjoying the sensation. And it made her plenty skittish, not to mention slower, on the way back as the bags slapped with each stride. Cowgirl pushed her forward all the same.

When they arrived back at the spot where Clemmy was down, they found Lizzy had been joined by several other riders who had come up behind on the trail. They had laid Clemmy flat and doused her with as much water as they still had. Now several of them were standing in a line, their bodies tight together, so they could create a small bit of shade for her.

Their heads lifted as Cowgirl rode up.

"We've got ice," is all Cowgirl had to say.

Cowgirl swung off Piper. Several riders were already walking toward her. Before long, they had the bags of ice unloaded. They used one bag as a kind of pillow, making sure as much of Clemmy's neck and head were in contact with the ice as possible. They packed the rest of it around her body, taking the cubes that slid off and mounding them back on top of her, holding other cubes against her wrists and neck in the spots where her superheated blood came closest to the surface. Clemmy, who seemed only dimly aware of what was happening, didn't object.

It took the EMTs twenty minutes to arrive. They had to walk the last few hundred feet with a stretcher. By the time they carried Clemmy off, she was already starting to come around. As she was loaded into the ambulance—a white Suburban—she was able to call out a request for someone to please take care of Chancellor.

The golden hour had gone her way.

The story was all around Michigan Bluff by the time Cowgirl and Lizzy arrived there. How the mother-daughter Tevis team had rescued a rider from certain danger at the top of El Dorado Canyon.

There were even cheers as Cowgirl and Lizzy entered the staging area. Piper, who was nothing if not a little bit of a drama queen, made the most of the moment. She held her head high, as if to prove that hauling eighty pounds of ice through the hot afternoon—and adding two extra miles onto a race that was already more than long enough—had been no big deal.

Lizzy waved at the people clapping. Cowgirl, businesslike as usual, just started looking for an available veterinarian.

Michigan Bluff is a full vet check, like the one at Robinson Flat—with all the poking and prodding and close inspection that goes with it. It's followed by an hour hold and Cowgirl was eager to get the clock started.

Most years, not as many horses get bounced out at Michigan Bluff, because the horses and riders that make it that far are generally in pretty good shape to start with.

But this was not most years. The heat was waging a war of attrition on the field. Of the 199 Tevis riders who had entered, only ninety were left. A few had come up lame, tied up, or were felled by natural obstacles. The rest were disqualified by the veterinarians who could be talked into bending a little on account of the heat, but could only bend so far. The horses were depending on them to make the right call.

Once a vet decides a horse is no longer fit to continue,

the vet might consult a colleague to make absolutely sure. Or the vet might not. Once the decision is made, it's final. There is no appeal process.

Still, I don't think Cowgirl was too worried. Piper and Jack had been eating and drinking well and generally showing good form.

Or at least she wasn't worried until she and Lizzy presented themselves, announced their numbers, and were instructed to ride over to the next free vet:

Vernon Puce.

In defiance of the heat and a long day that had started well before dawn, the old vet was looking just as cantankerous as ever. He had long ago discarded his bomber jacket and was now stripped down to his shirtsleeves, which confirmed that the only thing on his body more hairy than his nose and ears were his forearms.

"Well, well," he said, rubbing his hands together. "Look who it is."

"Hello," Cowgirl said thinly.

"I hear you had your Arab saving a VIP at El Dorado Canyon, that right?"

"Yep," she said. She had no idea why he was referring to Clemmy as a VIP. But Cowgirl wasn't about to ask Puce.

"Not sure that was the best idea, putting extra strain on your horse during a day like this," Puce opined.

He shook his head and sucked air through his teeth. Cowgirl just ground her molars. There was no point in saying anything that might provoke the man, who literally held her Tevis hopes in his liver-spotted hands.

Puce had already moved his gaze onto Lizzy.

"And how's L'il Miss Easy-on-the-Eyes doing?" Puce asked, running his tongue over his lips. "Getting tired, I imagine? I guess you're discovering the Tevis is no tea party, isn't that right, young lady?"

"Yep," Lizzy said.

"You been having any troubles? Awfully hot out there."

"No sir."

"That's a good girl," Puce said, then patted her chaps on the thigh.

He glanced back at Cowgirl who had fixed him with a look of contempt.

"I know, I know. You're going to tell me to mind the animals," Puce said. "Well, okay, let's get on with it then. Let's see those vet cards."

He started by taking pulses. Piper was sixty. Jack was fifty-eight. Puce offered no comment as he wrote the numbers down on the cards.

"All right," he said. "We got the yardage for Dr. Ridgeway's test marked out right over there. Why don't you go first there, L'il Miss Easy-on-the-Eyes, show your Momma how it's done."

Lizzy followed her instructions, trotting Jack out and back. Puce eyed Jack, whose gait couldn't have been more sound. A minute after Jack returned, Puce took the mule's pulse.

"Fifty-eight exactly," he said. "All right, big fella, hold still now."

Puce yanked up Jack's gums for the capillary refill test, checked his mucus membranes, tented the mule's neck and so on, going through the full list of required assessments. He finished by placing his stethoscope on Jack's stomach.

"All right," Puce said. "Everything seems to be fine with Mr. Long Ears here. I've got him checked in at"—he glanced at his watch—"five-o-one p.m. He'll be set to trot out again at six-o-one. Now, let's see how the Arab is doing."

Cowgirl trotted Piper out the required thirty-nine yards, then back again. Puce waited the minute required, then took the horse's pulse.

He looked up at Cowgirl and, with just the barest hint of a grin, said, "Sixty-six."

"What?!" Cowgirl said. Her hand immediately went down to the Arab's neck. "No it's not. It's sixty. I can tell by looking at her it's not more than sixty."

"You telling me I don't know how to count, woman?"

"Take it again."

"I got a lot of horses coming through after you. If I had to do every one of them twice, they'd be here all night. It's going on the card as a sixty-six, and that's the end of it."

His eyes were hard under his bushy eyebrows. A failed Dr. Ridgeway's test did not result in automatic disqualification. But it sure put a horse on the shortlist for one.

"Take it again," Cowgirl repeated.

"Too late now. It's been more than a minute."

"Fine. I'll trot out and back again."

"You'll stay right there and let me finish this examination, woman. And I don't want to hear another word otherwise."

Cowgirl's raised voice had garnered some attention in the vet area. A few heads turned their way, but then turned back. Puce was now mumbling to himself about women who didn't know their place.

He exposed Piper's gums and gave them a pinch.

"Capillary refill is a little on the slow side," he grumbled.

This time, it was Lizzy who spoke up, "There's no way that was more than a second."

Puce shot her an angry look. "Oh, now the child knows my business better than I do. Tell me, young lady, when did you attend veterinary school?"

Cowgirl was off her horse, standing straight and tall.

"Do it again," she demanded. "I want to see it."

Puce ignored her, made a mark on the card, and continued. With Cowgirl now hovering over him he went through the remaining battery of tests. Piper passed each one with no trouble until Puce reached out with his stethoscope.

Crouching near the horse's gut, he held it in one spot. Then he moved it to another.

"Awfully quiet in there," he said.

"It is not," Cowgirl said. "She's been eating just fine."

Paying no attention to her protest, Puce shifted the stethoscope again, then again.

Finally, he straightened, plucked the stethoscope out of his hairy ears, and shook his head as if he actually regretted the news he was about to deliver.

"I'm afraid this horse is showing real signs of metabolic distress," he said. "I can't, in good conscience, deem her fit to continue. I'm sorry, ma'am, but your race has come to an end."

"No!" Lizzy moaned. "No, you can't do that."

Cowgirl just stood there, hands on her hips, not saying a word. As a woman who had to spoon-feed her not-even-middle-aged husband every day, Cowgirl was familiar with the injustices the world could visit on a person. But this was beyond something she was quite ready for.

That after a year of training, after months of preparation, and after sixty-six miles of determined riding, her Tevis could be sacrificed on the altar of one man's spite.

And not just her Tevis. Lizzy's as well. There were only a few hours of daylight left. Most of the remaining ride would happen in darkness. Lizzy had never been on these trails before. It would be madness to send her out alone. Puce had gotten himself a two-for-one.

Well, three-for-one. If you count Cowboy as part of the team. And Cowgirl certainly did.

The vet just stood there, smugly, waiting for some reaction—most likely tears, since that's what he thought a woman would resort to under these circumstances. But Cowgirl wasn't going to give him that satisfaction. Even if, deep inside, a little bit of her had just died.

And then the expression on the Puce's face changed. In a less than a second, it went from self-satisfied, to surprised, to pained.

From seemingly out of nowhere, a huge right hand had landed on the spot where his shoulder met his neck. And it was squeezing. Hard.

A correspondingly large man was suddenly looming over Puce from behind.

"The horse stays in the race," Doc Jenson growled softly in his ear.

Puce was trying to turn around to face Jenson, but the bigger man wouldn't let him move. Puce began to protest, "Now, hold on a—"

"The horse stays," Jenson said again. "You know as well as I do there's not a horse in this field right now that's as fit to continue as this Arab here. And if you rule otherwise, Vernon, I'm going to find you stumbling out of that bar you like to visit some night, and I'm going to beat you so bad you'll never pee standing up again, you hear?"

Puce licked his lips. He still hadn't been able to turn around. Doc Jenson had planted his left hand on the other side of Puce's neck. Having headed the Tevis Vet Committee for years, Jenson knew him well. From a distance, it would have looked like Hitch Jenson was whispering sweet nothings in Vernon Puce's ear.

"And if you think I'm bluffing, just try me," Jenson continued. "I can't tell you how much satisfaction it would give me to ball you up and leave you crumpled in a dumpster somewhere."

Puce finally ripped himself away. He was trying to glare at Doc Jenson. But there's something about a glare that doesn't work so well when you have to crane your neck up that much.

"Fine," Puce spat. "But the numbers are staying on that card just the way I wrote them down. I'm not changing them."

Puce and Doc Jenson both knew the flunked Dr. Ridgeway's Test, as well as some of the low scores in the other areas, would probably cost Piper any shot she had at the Haggin Cup.

"You do what you have to do," Doc Jenson said. "You just write down that you cleared Piper here at five-o-five, and we'll call it a day. And don't you even think about catching up with these two at Francisco's or Pointed Rocks Ranch. If it's your turn when they come up, you're going to fake a stomach cramp."

"Go to hell, Hitch," Puce said.

"I might just do that," Doc Jenson replied. "But I swear if you come near these animals or these riders again, you'll get there first.

After attempting another glare, and failing just as badly as he did the first time, Puce stormed off.

When he was gone, Doc turned to Cowgirl and Lizzy.

"Sorry you had to hear that," he said.

"I'm not," Cowgirl said. "I wouldn't have wanted to miss a word."

Doc allowed himself a little bit of a smile, then said, "Let's go. We need to take care of these animals."

"Thanks, Hitch," Cowgirl said.

"Oh, I've been meaning to do that for years," Jenson said. "It's about time Vernon learns how to stop being an ass. Now come on."

Jenson led Cowgirl and Lizzy, who in turn led Piper and Jack, to the little camp the support team had set up. As soon as the animals were stopped, Doc and Choppy set about their work with Miss Betty assisting them.

Lizzy went straight to the cooler to prowl around for some candy bars, only to discover Miss Betty had found a new method of getting her way, there was only a turkey sandwich there waiting for her. But she quickly settled down with that and a cold water, too hungry and tired to do much complaining.

Cowgirl walked straight over to her husband who had a hat tilted over his face.

"Don't you go bothering him, now," Miss Betty said, before Cowgirl could say a word. "He went to sleep right before we got here. This heat's taken a lot out of him. If he's going to be awake to see you finish, it's good for him to rest now."

Cowgirl frowned. It wasn't like Cowboy to take a nap this late in the afternoon. She walked over toward him, likely to plant a kiss on his cheek. But Miss Betty separated herself from her task and ran at Cowgirl, blocking her access.

"Don't you dare," she said. "You just leave him be. That's nurse's orders."

Cowgirl didn't necessarily respect a nurse's orders. But she did respect Miss Betty.

Having been repelled, Cowgirl went to the cooler and plowed around until she found some venison jerky. Then, knowing she had no real job to do for the next hour, she walked off in the direction of the main tent.

Even Cowgirl was moving a bit stiffly by this point after a full day in the saddle. Other riders were in far worse shape. And as she walked toward the tent, Cowgirl saw her fellow competitors rubbing their legs, popping pain killers, guzzling water, or even catnapping in the shade. The horses clearly weren't the only animals being stretched to their limit.

Once she reached the tent, she walked toward the three large, moveable chalkboards that had been borrowed from a nearby elementary school and set up in the middle. There, in neat script, were the names of all the riders and horses that had passed through the vet check—along with the time they had come and left. It was the Tevis version of a scoreboard.

The very first names were Duke Dawson and his stallion Diesel. They had entered nearly an hour and a half earlier and were now gone. The second-place rider and horse were hot on their tails, three minutes behind. Third place was another minute after that. Then there was a pack of a dozen or so horses roughly ten minutes off the pace.

Cowgirl's eyes continued down to the end of the first

chalkboard without seeing her own name. She found Lizzy and herself midway down on the second chalkboard. They were in 47th and 48th place. Given how far back they had started, it was a respectable showing—and, more importantly, on pace to finish within twenty-four hours and win a buckle.

Still, if she felt any sense of hopefulness, she didn't show it. All she did was take a bite of the jerky she had been carrying. Optimism and Cowgirl appeared not well known to one another.

She kept going, reading the names of the ten teams that had come in behind them, looking for Woolfolk Henry and Laddy Boy. She reached the end without seeing them.

As she started back up at the top to look for Wooly's name again, a volunteer with a handheld radio walked up to another volunteer without one. Their conversation took place around a folding table less than ten feet from where Cowgirl was standing.

"So you heard the latest with the fire?" the one with the radio began.

"No. What?"

"It's heading toward the trail."

"Oh geez.

"It started somewhere north of Pilot Hill, but it's following the river up."

"Lot of trees on that side of the river. Lot of fuel."

"You know it. The Rangers say it's about four miles to the southwest of the trail, but it's heading northeast at about a mile an hour."

"So, in other words, it's going to get there in four hours."

"If it doesn't change course, yeah."

"Right about the time the leaders get there."

"I know. What do you think they're going to do?"

"I don't know. You can't exactly send riders into a forest fire."

"Think they'll hold them at Pointed Rocks?"

"Maybe. I'm just glad it's not going to be our call."

"You can say that again."

"Still, we should start letting the riders know what's going on. You take this side. I'll take that side. Meet you in the middle."

"Roger," the one with the radio finished.

Then both volunteers moved out.

Cowgirl took another bite of her jerky. There were times when I thought her lack of optimism went a little too far.

And there were other times when it seemed fully justified.

Chapter

20

Onward

AT PRECISELY 6:02 P.M., Cowgirl and Lizzy swung up into their saddles, so they could ride over to the vet area and be ready for release at 6:05.

There were no more full vet checks between Michigan Bluff and Auburn, just gate-and-goes; nor were there any spots where the support teams could access the course and cheer their riders on. This was the last time Cowgirl and Lizzy were going to see Doc, Miss Betty, Choppy and Cowboy until the finish line.

Choppy started off the goodbyes with, "Okay, you two. *Andale*. Ride like the wind."

"If only there *were* wind," Lizzy cracked.

Doc and Choppy both smiled. "Then maybe we should say 'Give e'm hell,'" Doc said.

"Yeah, there's plenty of that left out there," Lizzy said.

The men laughed. Cowgirl was shooting a few last anxious glances in the direction of Cowboy whose face was still partially shielded under the hat. Miss Betty was standing next to him, protectively, placing herself between Cowgirl and her husband in case she had any ideas about trying to kiss him again.

"Don't you worry about my friend here," Miss Betty

said. "He's just getting rested up for your big finish. I'm sure he'll be up when I move him back to the van but I want him to get a few more minutes rest while we pack up here."

Cowgirl looked like she wasn't convinced.

"He'll be fine," Miss Betty said, then made a shooing motion with both hands. "Now git on with you. Go on. Git. Git."

Knowing that was about as sentimental as a Miss Betty farewell was going to be, Cowgirl rode off with Lizzy behind her.

Choppy immediately got to work. He picked up the first of several loads destined for the vehicles and started off.

As soon as the riders were out of sight, Miss Betty released a huge sigh.

"What?" Doc asked.

"I thought that hour would never be up," she said.

Doc crinkled his forehead. Miss Betty lifted the hat off Cowboy's face.

He was wide awake. His eyes, which had been open for the entirety of the one-hour hold, had tears leaking out of them.

But that was not what immediately drew Doc's attention. It was Cowboy's lips, which were dusted white.

"He looks like you've been feeding him powdered donuts," Doc said.

"Yeah. It's called uremic frost," Miss Betty replied.

Doc again looked puzzled. "What's that?"

"It's another sign of end-stage kidney failure. Saw it in the hospital a few times. Once the kidneys give out, there's so much nitrogen that builds up in the body that little crystals of it start coming out in a patient's breath."

Doc studied Cowboy whose face was even more ashen than it had been in the morning.

"You think he'll make it to the finish line?" Doc asked.

"No. But I didn't think he was going to make it to the

Tevis this year in the first place. So that shows what I know."

"Shouldn't we tell Cowgirl?" Doc asked, his eyes going toward the vet area where she was still waiting.

"Don't you even think about it. She'll just make noises about quitting again."

"Would that really be the worst thing?" Doc asked.

Miss Betty balled up her wrinkled face. "Whose side are you on, anyway?"

"I'm just asking the question."

Miss Betty hefted an exasperated sigh. "You know how long it's been since that girl's had her nails done?"

"What's that got to do with anything?"

"Eight years," Miss Betty continued. "She used to go all the time. You look at any picture of her from back in her rodeo days, and she always had the most beautiful red nails, always freshly done, never a chip on 'em. Nowadays? They look like they've been chewed by bears."

"Okay, and?"

"And she doesn't go shopping. And she doesn't read books. I can't even get her to eat a proper dinner most nights."

"I'm not sure I get your point."

"My point is, that girl never does anything for herself. Everything is about her husband, or her daughter, or her pie business, or me, or some stray that's wandered in off the street. This is the one exception she makes. The Tevis. Dreaming of the Tevis. Training for the Tevis. Prepping for the Tevis. Talking about how much it would mean for her husband to see Lizzy and her finish the Tevis. That's it. That's all she's got.

"And for as much as you and I think it's going to be a blessing when he finally moves on, the fact is that girl is going to be in a world of hurt. It's no fun burying the person you thought you were going to spend the rest of your days with. So before that happens, I want her to have this. I want her to have this all to herself, without you, or my friend here"—she gestured at Cowboy—"or anything else getting in the way. I want her to have that one wonderful moment."

From underneath all the folds of her face, Miss Betty's eyes were misty.

She had no more words to say.

And I think maybe, looking at those eyes, Doc finally got it. That it was about Cowgirl getting a wonderful moment with her family, yes. But it was also about Miss Betty, and the moment she never got with her own.

"Okay," is all Doc said.

"Good man," Miss Betty said, her voice faltering just a little. "Now hush up and get back to work."

Choppy took a long time coming back for his second load. Doc, who was nearly done with breaking down the camp by that point, looked up, curious.

"Where have you been?"

"Just had something to take care of," Choppy said.

Doc looked at him quizzically but left it at that. Together they made short work of what little remained—the horses having toted off most of it in their stomachs. Miss Betty busied herself with Cowboy who let out one or two moans, though they didn't seem to signify much of anything.

Once she finished loading him, Doc and Choppy hopped in Doc's truck, and the two-vehicle convoy started on their way toward the Auburn Fairgrounds and McCann Stadium, where they hoped, many hours from now, they would get to see Cowgirl and Lizzy complete their triumph.

But before they left the parking area, they passed two ranch hands, one with a straw hat, the other wearing a cap from a feed store. They were shouting and carrying on, taking in huge mouthfuls of water and then spitting them out.

"What's gotten into them?" Doc asked.

"I don't think their beer tastes so good," Choppy replied, a small grin on his face.

"What makes you say that?"

"I spiked it with horse piss."

Chapter

21

Darkness

THE THIRD OF THE KILLER CANYONS that trisects the Tevis course is the one that dips down to Volcano Creek.

I couldn't tell you why the creek got that name. Maybe it's just because by that point on the trail, the riders feel like they're ready to erupt.

Volcano Creek is not as steep as Swinging Bridge Canyon. It's not as deep El Dorado. What it does have is that the first canyons have pretty much knocked the stuffing out of both horse and rider, making them wonder if they can really do it one more time. Not that there's much choice.

So they traversed through more switchbacks; down more narrow, rocky trails; past more drop offs that made even the stoutest stomach get quaky.

I think it helped that Lizzy was so fatigued she couldn't work up as much distress as she did early on when she was fresher. She just kept clinging to Jack, trusting her mule to do the work.

They spoke sparingly. Every now and then, Cowgirl would say, "Watch out for that." Or, if she felt like Jack was trying to push the pace too much, she'd say, "Ease off there." Or Lizzy would say, "Let's run this part," and they'd slide out of their saddles and take to their feet.

At the bottom of the canyon, the animals waded into the creek and drank, letting the water fill their bellies and cool their hot muscles. Then it was back up the other side.

The upward climbing switchbacks can only be traveled at two speeds: slow and slower. And it was here, during all that repetitive monotony, that Cowgirl finally started to find the words for the thoughts that had been working their way through her mind for a few hours now, ever since Lizzy had spewed her anger at Devil's Thumb.

She might have waited until they got home to have this conversation. But there was something about the Tevis that required they have it now. Maybe it was because the ride was going to place so many more demands on them, they simply couldn't survive it together unless the air was cleared.

Or maybe it was because of the spirit that lingered over the route itself. You have to remember who first carved the Western States Trail. The 49ers weren't men who were leaving behind prosperous farms or successful businesses. They were men who had struggled somewhere else and were now going out to California—to that rugged, strange and uncertain world—because it gave them the hope that all that gold in them thar hills could fix everything else in their lives that had gone awry.

In other words, the Western States Trail has been offering broken people a fresh start for a long time now. And that's what I think Cowgirl was looking for, midway up the wall of that last canyon, when she cleared her throat and spoke.

"You blame me, don't you," Cowgirl said.

"For what?" Lizzy said.

"For your hand."

Lizzy rode in silence for a moment. The only noise came from the crunching of Jack's hooves grinding in the loose dirt and rock.

"I don't know," she said, at last.

"It was my horse who did it."

"I know."

"I never told you Piper didn't rail tie and that she would rear and pull back when tied to a rail or anything else."

"I know."

"We were only going for a ride that day because of me. I wanted Jack to have another chance to get used to you on a long ride. To build your endurance. And his. If it wasn't for me and the Tevis, you never would have even been near the barn that day. You probably would have been inside practicing."

"I know," Lizzy said for a third time.

"Once it happened, I guess I got so wrapped up in the medical stuff—what was going to happen to your finger, what was the best course to take, where should we get the surgery done that I didn't...I didn't revisit the accident. It was just full speed ahead, don't look back."

"Like usual," Lizzy said.

Cowgirl took a moment to absorb that comment, then said, "Yes, like usual. So please give me a chance now. What I'm saying is, it's okay if you blame me. And I'm sorry. I really, really am sorry. There are no words or at least words I can come by easily. Maybe I haven't told you that enough because I blame myself, too. It's been a tough thing for me to come to grips with. As a mother, it's difficult to think that my dream cost my daughter her dream. That's not how it's supposed to go."

Cowgirl tried to turned around and look at Lizzy, to get some read on what her daughter was thinking. But it was not such an easy thing, being that her eyes also needed to stay on the trail ahead of them. As fine a horse as Piper was, she still needed the rider.

"It broke my heart too, you know," Cowgirl said, once she was facing forward again. "I know how much it meant to you. It meant a lot to me, too. You know that, right?"

There was still nothing coming from behind Cowgirl

other than the sound of a mule doing hard work.

Finally, Lizzy said, "Mom, can we just ride?"

"Sure," she said.

And so ride they did. Every time there was a switchback that gave her the chance, Cowgirl caught a glance at her daughter.

There was a time—when Lizzy was an infant, a toddler, and even a little girl—that she could not have hidden the slightest thought from her mother even if she wanted to. The younger Lizzy had one of those faces that gave away what was going through the brain behind it almost instantly. If Lizzy was scared, her brow pinched. If Lizzy was happy, her cheeks lit up. If Lizzy was determined, her mouth would go in a straight line, her upper lip sucked in just a little.

That time had passed. Now all Cowgirl saw on each switchback was a mask that hid the thoughts behind it—a mask as hard and impenetrable as the canyon walls surrounding them.

Once they completed their climb out of Volcano Creek Canyon, Cowgirl and Lizzy reached one of the few reprieves the Tevis offers its riders.

Coming out of Volcano Creek Canyon, the trail dead-ends at the shoulder of a wide road, which then slopes down into Foresthill, California.

The main street of the small town is patterned after Market Street in San Francisco. But no one is likely to confuse the two—there are no cable cars in Foresthill, no sea lions lolling on nearby piers—but it has a nice wide strip of grass that the animals can trot down.

That's not what makes it a treat though. The real fortifying factor is the hospitality of all the people there. Pretty much the whole town comes out. Or at least it feels that way. And after seventy miles, most of which is wilderness and sweat, it can be nice to have some total strangers cheering you on.

In addition to the shouts and claps, there were signs that said, "Welcome Tevis Riders!" Or "Keep it up!" Or "30 miles to Auburn!" I don't think there is a Tevis participant—rider or mount—who goes through that town without a little grin on their face.

Cowgirl certainly was smiling. Piper was trotting along, tail high, the Arab equivalent of a smile. Jack had the satisfaction of certain people signaling him out for applause—there are fans of mules everywhere you go. Even Lizzy perked up when some of the spectators recognized she was the youngest competitor in the field and gave her a little extra encouragement.

The only trouble with Foresthill is that it's over so quickly. From there, it's back into the woods, up over Baltimore Mine Ridge, over Dardanelles Creek, and toward the Middle Fork of the American River which the trail then follows for several miles.

One of the significant landmarks is Ruck-A-Chucky Falls, a cascade created by a huge landslide that went across the American River sometime in the distant past. Ruck-A-Chucky is magnificent in both sight and sound—all that water tumbling over all those boulders, all that frothing and rushing and seething—though I'm not sure a Tevis rider can really take the time to appreciate it.

They're simply spent, some sixteen hours after they first swung up on their mount in the predawn chill of Squaw Valley. They're feeling that saddle wearing on them in ways it never does during a training ride. Their horse's back has probably never seemed so wide. Lastly, they're focused on the trail and on the work at hand. By that point in the ride, the miles are really clicking by. And so is the clock. The sun is very low in the sky and shadows are growing long.

To a first-timer like Lizzy it would have seemed like a blessing. The sinking sun takes the worst of the heat with it.

An eighty degree twilight feels positively balmy after the searing heat of the canyons.

But the veterans know it's a mixed blessing. Because it signifies the next great challenge of the Tevis is approaching.

If the first section is defined by mountains, and the second is distinguished by canyons, the third and final part of the Tevis is memorable and difficult for one primary reason.

The darkness.

And as Cowgirl and Lizzy began the long, slick, downhill switchback that follows Ruck-A-Chucky Falls, it was coming on fast.

To the horses, the dark is really nothing, of course. Horses have huge eyes with pupils that can dilate until they're the size of quarters and beyond, allowing the ambient light to pour in.

It's that evolution thing again. Way back when, many of the predators who liked to snack on horse flesh hunted at night. The horse that couldn't see well enough to run away was not likely to pass on its genes to the next generation.

No, it's really the humans who have the problem. While the ancestral horses were on the plains, running through the night, we were somewhere safe, snoozing. There just wasn't as much of a need for our kind to make out shapes in the shadows. As long as we stayed where it was safe.

I think that's what makes the night so forbidding to our species. We've got millions of years of training telling us to hunker down and not head out until the sun comes back up.

But, of course, anyone who wants to complete a hundred miles in one day doesn't really have that choice.

Chapter

22

The Work

AS THEY NEARED FRANCISCO'S gate-and-go, eighty-five long and weary miles into the race, Cowgirl reined back Piper to a walk, forcing Jack to do the same.

It was because she knew the animals would need to get their heartbeats down, yes; but it was also something else.

Something ominous in the air.

"You smell that?" Lizzy asked, as her mother slowed.

"Yep," Cowgirl said.

"I've been getting it for a few miles now."

It was the sharp, pitchy, sooty scent of a forest fire. And the wind, which had been picking up steadily since the sun went down, was carrying it ever closer.

"You think it's getting near the trail?" Lizzy asked.

"Don't know," Cowgirl said. She hadn't told Lizzy about what she had overheard at Michigan Bluff. "Guess we'll find out."

They got their answer soon enough. As soon as they arrived at the-gate-and go, they were met by the sight of a half-dozen trucks, each of them with a horse trailer hitched behind. They were being bathed in a sodium halide glow by a temporary light stanchion, which was being powered by a portable diesel generator.

It spit out enough brightness that Cowgirl and Lizzy could see two horses, waiting to be loaded.

After handing their cards over to a veterinarian and verifying that Piper and Jack were below the sixty-four-beat-per-minute threshold, they were approached by a volunteer. He had to raise his voice slightly to be heard over the chattering of the generator's engine.

"Evening," he said.

"Evening," Cowgirl returned.

"I take it you've heard about the fire."

"Yep."

"Well, the latest is that it's growing, and it's coming towards us. The Rangers are telling us there is a better-than-ninety percent chance the fire is going to overtake the trail within the next hour and it doesn't look like there's going to be anything that'll put it out. There's still a lot of fuel out there for it to burn through. The projected path has it going near the Pointed Rocks Ranch vet check. Right between the gate-and-go there and No Hands Bridge. We've already evacuated all vehicles from Pointed Rocks Ranch, because there's a danger the roads could be cut off. There are a few volunteers left who are there on horseback, but they're on orders to get out if the fire comes much closer. We're in touch with them via radio, so they have the latest reports from the Rangers. Of course, we've eliminated the gate-and-go there."

"Roger," Cowgirl said.

"What we've been instructed to tell the riders is that we can't guarantee their safety if they choose to go on after this point. Once you cross the river, we have no way of getting you out. They've already closed down Highway 49 to vehicle traffic.

"Also," he continued. "We've been informed by the power company that they had to release the dam just up river. We fought them on it. But they said they didn't have a choice. So there's some pretty high water at Poverty Bar this year. If your horse can't swim..."

The volunteer looked towards the fleet of trucks and stock trailers assembled. "That's what those are for. We can get you out on Old Greenwood Bridge Road and then up to Foresthill Road, which can take you safely into Auburn, where you can meet up with your support crew. We're just going to shuttle back and forth, so there should be room for anyone who wants to take us up on the offer."

"If we take the trailer, do we still get a buckle?" Lizzy asked.

"Afraid not, young lady."

"And if we choose to go on?" Cowgirl asked.

"Then you still have a shot at a buckle," he said. "But at that point, you're on your own."

Cowgirl nodded. Underneath her, Piper shifted her weight.

"How many people have chosen the trailers?" Cowgirl asked.

"A little more than half."

"Duke Dawson go through?"

"He sure did. Dawson and a few of the other leaders passed through here in a hot hurry more than an hour ago. I think they were hoping to sneak through before the fire cut them off."

"Any idea if they made it?"

"They haven't checked in at Pointed Rocks Ranch yet, so they're running short on time if they want to. Sounds like it's going to be real tight."

Something squawked on the man's radio. He brought the radio close to his ear and frowned as he listened to the squelchy voice for a minute or so.

"Just another report from the Rangers," he said. "Sounds like the Hotshots are hard at work making a fire line, but only on the Auburn side of the river. They're not doing anything on our side."

From the distance, someone shouted a question at the volunteer. He hollered back, "Be right there."

Then he turned his attention to Cowgirl and Lizzy. "Anyhow, you gals let us know what you want to do. We're keeping a list of who goes on, so we can make sure everyone's accounted for. But there's plenty of room in the trailers, too. It's up to you. Just make sure you see me either way."

He gave a curt nod, stuffed his handheld radio in his belt and walked back toward the trailers. It left Cowgirl and Lizzy alone in the semi-darkness.

"Well, what do you think?" Cowgirl asked.

"I don't know," Lizzy said. "What do you think?"

It was rather like a teenager to be full of opinions until you actually want them to have one. Cowgirl took a deep breath and let it out slowly.

"I'm pretty sure Jack has never swum before," she said. "I think Piper has. But that was before she came to us. Between that and the fire..."

Cowgirl let that dangle and twist for a moment, like she wanted to hear how it sounded spoken out loud so she could consider it a little more.

Then she came back with renewed force, saying, "I think I've pushed you far enough. Too far, actually."

"Who says you're pushing me?" Lizzy said.

"Oh, Lizzy. I've been pushing and dragging you with this Tevis stuff since well before you hurt your hand. It's time for me to stop. If your broken finger wasn't the sign that it was time, then the combination of a fire and a flood certainly is."

"Eighty-five miles is a long way to go and not get a buckle, Mom."

"Yeah, but there's always next year."

Suddenly Lizzy got a look about her. It was a look Cowgirl recognized from long ago. Lizzy's mouth was a straight line. Her upper lip was sucked in.

And then she said: "Not for Dad, there's not."

Cowgirl had no response.

"This was what he always talked about," Lizzy said. "For our family to finish the Tevis together."

"I'm always telling you: dreams have a way of changing," Cowgirl said.

"Well, this one hasn't," Lizzy responded.

Without another word, Lizzy touched her heels to Jack's side and steered him toward the volunteer with the radio.

"Hi, sir, I'm wondering: what goes faster, a mule or a forest fire?"

The man looked up.

"Excuse me?"

"What goes faster, a mule or a forest fire?"

"Well, I would say a mule, but—"

"Then please mark down in your list than one-eighty-eight and one-eighty-nine have decided to go on."

"Okay," he said, bringing the radio to his lips and reporting that news.

Lizzy urged Jack forward again, toward the place where the trail resumed. Cowgirl had to canter Piper to catch up.

"Hey, wait. Just wait. Are you sure about this?"

Lizzy reined Jack back just short of the trailhead. She turned toward Piper and Cowgirl. The light of the gate-and-go, now distant, cast only the slightest glow on Lizzy's face.

"You were ready to quit at Devil's Thumb," Cowgirl said. "And for whatever you might think, I was actually fine with it."

"I was just hot and cranky."

"Well, I know. But, look, you don't have to do this. Not for me. Not for Dad. We'll be okay no matter what happens."

"I know you will."

"So come on then. Let's just get Piper and Jack loaded up in and be done with this."

Cowgirl touched the reins to the left side of Piper's neck, telling her to make a right turn—in the direction of trailers. But Lizzy held firm.

"I'm not totally doing this for you and Daddy," she said.

Cowgirl gave Piper a soft tug. The horse stopped.

"I've been thinking a lot while we've been riding," Lizzy said. "And I didn't want to say anything because it seemed, well, I was still trying to figure it all out. But…I think the reason I was so sad and so angry after I mashed my finger is because without the violin, I didn't know what my dream was anymore. And I know you say dreams have a way of changing. But, really, what else did I have? It's not like there's anything in Lodi. My music…my violin…was everything to me."

"Sweetheart—"

"But I think, I don't know, I keep thinking about something Daddy always used to tell me. He always said that each day his goal was to do the best work he could do until the work was all done."

"'To do the best work in the world that we can do till the best we can do is all done," Cowgirl said, quoting from memory.

"Yeah, that. And, you know, if you follow that...maybe there's not just one dream. Maybe there's a different dream every day, you know? Or not every day. But there's definitely a whole lot of dreams out there. And they're going to change, and change, and change again. And maybe what really matters is just that you keep working toward them."

Jack's candlestick ears gave a twitch.

"So that's why we're going to keep going," Lizzy continued. "Not because it's your dream or my dream or Daddy's dream. But because the work isn't done."

She nodded her head and repeated, "The work isn't done,

Mom. Not for another fifteen miles."

Cowgirl was sitting perfectly straight in her saddle.

"Your father," she said, "would be so proud to hear you say that. Maybe you'll tell him that when we get to Auburn?"

"You mean when we get to Auburn on Jack and Piper. Not in a trailer. Right?"

"Yep."

"Then yeah, I'll tell him."

"And I want you to know something," Cowgirl said. "Whatever your dream is, I'm there with you."

"I know, Mom…I know." Lizzy said softly.

Chapter

23

American River

IT'S ROUGHLY THREE MILES from Francisco's down to Poverty Bar, where the Western States Trail crosses the Middle Fork of the American River for the first time.

Any hint of sunset was now completely gone from the sky, but the full moon was rising in its place, filling the trail with its pale glow. At this point, most Tevis riders slow it down, put on their headlamps or snap a glow stick and attach it to the breast plate of their horse, relying on those artificial sources of light to strike upon any dangers in time for them to steer their horses out of the way.

Not Cowgirl and Lizzy. Piper and Jack had done most of their Tevis training at night—or, technically, early morning—the only time when Cowgirl's schedule allowed. They were almost more accustomed to darkness than they were to daylight. Nighttime was their time.

To me, there's always been a certain magic about riding in darkness. The ground is more of a rumor, and the horse just seems to fly along beneath you, its hooves beating out a rhythm that you can somehow tune in to easier. The connection between horse and rider is as if two are one. You see less, but you feel more. And feeling is always far more important when you're in the saddle.

There were few riders on the trail now. Only eighty teams out of the original 199 had made it as far as Francisco's. And only thirty-five of those had ultimately decided to go on. Those thirty-five were stretched out over many miles, meaning Cowgirl and Lizzy had that darkness all to themselves.

They rode at a good clip. The trail more or less follows the river for all of those ten miles, and their ears kept giving them reminders of the challenge they were soon to face.

The Middle Fork of the American River has its headwaters in the Granite Chief Wilderness Area up at about 8,000 feet. After merging with the North Fork near Auburn, the river ends at Folsom Lake, at an elevation of about 500 feet. It makes that 7,500-foot drop in just 63 miles. Compare that to the Mississippi River, which begins at 1,500-feet and takes 2,320 miles to work its way to sea level, and you start to understand just how powerful the Middle Fork of the American River is.

Back before the river was dammed, when it was still wild and untamed, it rushed by so fast—and made so much noise doing it—miners who approached it often thought they were hearing thunder. Especially during the spring melt, when a winter's worth of snowflakes were making their way down the river at the same time, creating that rumbling roar. The miners would look around on April mornings, bewildered as to where the storm could possibly be coming from. They eventually coined a phrase to describe that trick of sound: bogus thunder.

Ordinarily, by the middle of summer, the bogus thunder has quieted. Most years, Tevis riders who ford the American River at Poverty Bar do so in water that doesn't rise much past their horse's knees.

Except, of course, by releasing the dam when it did, the power company had essentially created a spring melt in August. The edges of the river, the shallower parts, had turned into roiling rapids. But that wasn't nearly as treacherous as the middle, which was now deep enough that the water was rushing over it without so much as a ripple. It was just dark and smooth and deadly.

As Cowgirl and Lizzy rode down toward the riverbank, they saw four riders, swinging up into their saddles.

But not to cross the river. They had their horses pointed in the opposite direction.

"Hey there," Cowgirl called out. "What's going on?"

A man with a headlamp blazing trotted over to Cowgirl, semi-blinding her, making it impossible for her to see his face.

"River's just too high," he said. "We talked it over for a while and we've decided it's too dangerous. Maybe during the day. But not at night."

"How deep do you think it is?" Cowgirl asked.

"Well, that's the problem, isn't it? We don't know. But I think the middle of that channel is probably eight to ten feet right now, over our heads for sure. I think it's madness to even try."

He then offered a few choice words for the power company. "Anyhow, our little posse here has been going together since Michigan Bluff, but we've decided we're done. No belt buckle is worth risking your life."

"So where are you going?" Cowgirl asked.

"I know a trail that'll take us up to Foresthill Road," he said. "Once we're there, we're going to flag down one of the trailers going to or from Francisco's. It's not more than a mile or two. Come with us, if you want to."

Cowgirl turned to Lizzy, who had heard everything the man had said. Cowgirl was about to open her mouth and speak, then stopped herself.

She didn't need to ask the question. All it took was one glance at Lizzy's face. Even in the shadows, Cowgirl could see her daughter had come too far—and overcome too much—to possibly turn back now.

"No thanks," Cowgirl said. "I think we're going to give it a shot."

"You sure?"

This time Cowgirl didn't even bother looking at Lizzy. She just said, "Yep."

"All right," the man said. "Can't say I agree with you, but good luck. If you change your mind, just holler. We'll wait for you."

"Thanks," Cowgirl said.

The four horses trotted past them. Cowgirl gave Piper a squeeze, and they went down to the banks of the river with Lizzy and Jack right behind.

Cowgirl dismounted and began tucking in all the bits of her gear and tack that might interfere with Piper's swimming, taking extra care to make sure nothing would get in the way of her front legs. Lizzy was doing the same without being told.

Once Cowgirl was done, she looked over at her daughter. "You ready?"

"Not quite yet," Lizzy said. Then she went around and reached into her saddlebag, pulling out a small, brown object.

"Okay, Jenny, I've been saving you for when I really needed you," she said. "And I think we could use all the luck you can give us right now."

She patted the toy mule, then kissed it.

"Mom?" she said, holding out Jenny.

"Oh, why not?" Cowgirl said, then walked over and gave Jenny a tiny pat.

Lizzy took one glance at the south bank, looking ghostly in the moonlight, 120 feet and one angry river away. Then she returned Jenny to her saddlebag.

"Okay," Lizzy said. "*Now* I'm ready."

As the river roared below them, Cowgirl and Lizzy pulled up into their saddles. They walked Piper and Jack up to the edge, where the bogus thunder echoed.

"So how do we do this?" Lizzy shouted.

"Jack may never have swum before," Cowgirl said. "So remember: we don't know quite how he's going to react."

"He's Jack. He'll be fine, right?"

"Well, he'll be fine, yes. Mules are born knowing how to swim. It's you I worry about. I think you guys should go first so I can keep an eye on you."

"Jack won't like that," Lizzy said, looking uncertain.

"He'll have to deal with it," Cowgirl said. "The river is going to carry us downstream quite a bit, but that's fine. The trail follows the river for a while, so we'll be able to climb the bank and meet up with it. The whole thing is to just keep working toward the other side, no matter what. Don't battle the current. You won't win. Even though you took that first in the junior freestyle three years ago at the Lodi pool. "

"Okay."

"And make sure you keep your feet out of the stirrups. So if your dumped off you won't get trapped under him." You might actually float a bit because of the current. Hold tight as you can to his mane."

"Okay."

"But don't get dumped."

"Got it."

"Great. Okay. You can do it."

"I know," Lizzy said.

She gave Jack a squeeze, and his hooves went into the water. His steps were tentative. The big mule didn't like to go first. He had spent a year leading Piper from behind, and he liked it that way. He wasn't keen on Piper being out of his sight.

"Come on, boy," Lizzy said. "It's just water. You like water."

She squeezed a little harder, and in Jack went. There was no droop to his eyes now. They were wide open.

The river rushed past his pasterns, then his knees, the water swirling and creating tiny whirlpools on the downstream side of his legs. He was taking slow, careful strides, like he still wasn't sure about all this.

"Let's go," Lizzy said. "We're wasting time."

Behind them, Lizzy was aware Cowgirl and Piper had entered the water. But she didn't look back. Her focus had to be entirely forward.

The footing was relatively solid. Poverty Bar was the preferred crossing point of the river for that reason. There were no big boulders to worry about. Still, Jack swayed slightly as he got deeper and the full force of the river slammed into his broadside.

"It's okay, big fella, you're all right," Lizzy said, patting his neck.

Lizzy yelped a little as the water first hit her feet and filled her sneakers.

For now she was freezing. As hot as she had been earlier in the day, the American River is fed by glaciers. Even in mid-July, even after it's made the long trip to Poverty Bar, the water temperature doesn't get much above the mid-sixties. It quickly covered her thighs.

Jack kept plodding along as the water rose to his shoulders, feeling his way one step at a time. His long ears were pinned back now like he meant business. It was all going fine as long as there was still gravel under his hooves.

The trouble came when he took his first step that didn't find the riverbed.

As Cowgirl said, most mules are born swimmers. The good part about that is they naturally stay afloat. The bad part is how they do it. As soon as they come up empty on that one step—hitting only water instead of something solid—their necks immediately crane up, almost like a periscope. It's a self-preservation instinct, the animal doing what it has to do to keep its head above water.

Lizzy didn't know it was coming, of course. Her fists were clenched with hands-full of Jack's mane. But, as soon as his big head and neck craned up, she was knocked loose as she lost her grip.

From perhaps fifteen feet behind, Cowgirl could only watch as Jack's sudden move, combined with the current, launched Lizzy loose.

"Lizzy!" Cowgirl shouted.

But her daughter had disappeared under the dark surface of the river swirl, with not even a ripple to mark where she had gone.

"Lizzy!" Cowgirl shouted again to no greater effect. "Lizzy!"

Jack was still battling along. He was now swimming strongly, working toward the south shore, which was another eighty feet away. If he knew he had dumped Lizzy, he gave no sign of it.

Cowgirl scanned the water, desperately looking for some sign of her daughter. A shoe. A leg. Something to show Lizzy had surfaced and was thrashing toward dry land. Cowgirl had to fight the urge to fling herself off Piper and dive into the river and look for Lizzy, a move that would have been as dangerous as it was futile. There was truly nothing Cowgirl could do.

If there is a more desperate thing than the helplessness of a mother who knows her child is in mortal danger and can't do anything about it, I don't know what it is.

"Lizzy," she cried. "Lizzy!"

An over whelming frantic and terrible dread were welling up in her.

"Help," she yelled. "Someone, help us!"

But there was no answer. There was no one, there in the middle of the Middle Fork of the American River, in the dark of night, to hear her plea. No matter how many times she bellowed her daughter's name, no matter what desperate prayer she offered, it didn't change that Lizzy was gone.

The only thing that got Cowgirl to the other side of the channel was that Piper kept swimming, oblivious to the drama. The Arab had no intention to stop in the middle of the river and look for anyone.

As soon as Piper's hooves struck solid ground, Cowgirl rolled off her horse and began wading around in the dark deep water. The current was still enormously strong. But Cowgirl's resolve to find her daughter was stronger.

"Lizzy!" she yelled. "Lizzy!"

Cowgirl's gaze swept over the middle of the river, up and down, still aching for anything that resembled a teenage girl. Perhaps a glimpse of her blond head or a fair-skinned arm stroking a strong freestyle.

But there was nothing. Cowgirl called and called again. Her face was wet from the river, wet from her tears. Pure agony was settling into her stomach.

And then, from behind her, she heard the three of the sweetest words to ever grace her ears.

"Over here, Mom."

Halfway between Cowgirl and the shore, standing in water up to her thighs, was Lizzy—sopping and bedraggled but otherwise fine. Cowgirl surged toward her, her thighs slicing through the thick water like it was barely there.

"Oh, Lizzy," Cowgirl said. "Baby."

When she reached Lizzy, Cowgirl hugged her fiercely.

"Mom, take it easy," Lizzy said. "Come on. When you taught me to swim, you always said how it might save my life someday."

"I know, I know. But...when you vanished I thought..."

She didn't say the words. She couldn't. The thought was altogether too dreadful, even now that it wasn't going to come true.

"I'm not a little kid any more, Mom. I'll be fine. You don't always need to be watching me."

"But a part of me always will be," Cowgirl said.

"I know, Mom, I know."

Cowgirl went to release the hug, but Lizzy only let her get so far. She grasped her mother's wrists and held them so she couldn't get away. She held them with a firmness that surprised Cowgirl; a strength that hinted this teenage girl was going to be a strong woman one day, just like her Momma.

"Wait, Mom. There's been something I've been wanting to say," Lizzy said.

She gathered the thought for a moment, then said, "It was the horse, Mom."

"What are you talking about?"

"It was Piper who mashed my finger. Not you. I get that now. And I...I really don't blame you. Maybe I did at first, but not anymore."

"Lizzy, I—"

"It was the horse. That's all there is to say."

Cowgirl studied her for a long moment, nodded, then said, "Yep."

Then they walked up the river bank, arm in arm under the full moon.

Chapter

24
Window

IT WAS CLOSING IN ON MIDNIGHT now, and Cowgirl and Lizzy had either been in the saddle—or oh-so-briefly out of it—for nineteen hours.

Lizzy was sore beyond anything she had experienced in her fourteen years, with an ache in her seat that cut through the muscle and bone and went straight up her spine. She had Jack going at a good trot and the mule's every bounce radiated from her seat up to the base of her skull and then back down again. Only her youth, and the gumption she inherited from both sides of her family tree kept her going.

Even Cowgirl was hurting a little. Not that she would have admitted it. She had brought back out her fringed jacket, which had stayed dry in its waterproof pouch, to help ward off the chill that had settled in after the plunge into the river.

This is ordinarily a quiet time in the Tevis, a time of pain and exhaustion, a time when the riders' attention tends to flag and their eyelids droop.

Yet this being no ordinary Tevis, Cowgirl and Lizzy were strangely awake. Sharp even.

There was just an ominous feeling in the air. That, and a lot of smoke.

What had started as a small brush fire, touched off by a lightning strike many hours earlier, had now turned into a raging conflagration that had consumed thousands of acres.

The smell of it grew stronger as they continued east and slightly south, still following the river, but now on the other side. Conifers have a particular scent when they burn, as all that sap inside gets incinerated. The heat turns it into tiny molecules that then take it into the atmosphere, floating along until they settle in an unsuspecting person's nose many miles later. And that's what Cowgirl and Lizzy were now breathing in: little pieces of the fire char itself.

The sky, once so clear, had grown hazy, obscuring the moon in a gauzy blur. Stars that had once been strong enough to almost outshine the moonlight were now completely gone.

Before long the western horizon began to get an eerie orange glow about it. It was faint at first. But it became brighter as they pressed toward it. It was like a setting sun they could somehow catch up to. The animals were clearly aware of the change in conditions. Like I said, equines are Einsteins when it comes to sensing hazard.

Piper was getting agitated, constantly jerking her head to the side, forcing Cowgirl to take a heavier hand on the reins than she ordinarily would have liked.

Jack, if anything, got even calmer than usual, like he had this sense of purpose about him. Maybe it's just that a mule knows when humans are riding toward trouble, he's going to be the one to get them out of it.

After a few miles, as the smoke grew thicker still, Cowgirl stopped Piper, went to her saddlebag, and pulled out a bandana. She tied it around her nose and mouth, to act as a kind of filter. Lizzy did the same. They looked like a pair of bandits.

They were still wearing them a short time later when, about three miles short of Pointed Rocks Ranch, they were met by the peculiar sight of a man standing in the middle of the trail, waving a pair of flashlights to his left like he was directing a commercial airliner.

"This way, this way," he said. "Trail's closed. Towards the river. That's right. Towards Browns Bar, that way."

Browns Bar is nothing more than a sandbar in the middle of the American River. To the south side of it is an open meadow that riders would ordinarily pass by in the dark without even noticing in their push toward the finish.

Which made it especially strange to see twenty-odd horses crowding the area. Some had blankets on. Some were grazing. Others were drinking from the river. Others were tied to trees by their halter ropes.

None were being ridden.

The riders were similarly arrayed in small groups, or sitting, or just wandering about aimlessly. The whole scene was so lacking in anything resembling organization it left Cowgirl hesitant about what, exactly, she and her daughter were supposed to do.

Her uncertainty was interrupted when a tall, slender man with a handheld radio walked over to greet them.

"Good evening," he said in a genial manner that belied the strangeness of the circumstances. "I'm Hal Chambers. I'm the race director."

It spoke to the urgency of the situation that the race director, who typically would stay at Auburn to coordinate the finish, had felt compelled to join this oddly assembled collection of riders by the side of the American River.

"Good evening," Cowgirl said. "We're one-eighty-eight and one-eight-nine."

"Great. Can I have your vet cards, please?"

Cowgirl and Lizzy reached into their saddle bags, pulled them out, and handed them to Chambers.

"The mother-daughter team," he said. "We heard you were coming. Glad you made it across the river."

"So are we. Thanks."

"Well, as you can probably tell, we've had to hold the riders here," Chambers said. We have fires before on race day and we've managed. But right now the fire has overtaken the trail to the west of here. We had to evacuate Pointed Rocks Ranch about two hours ago, before the first riders even got there. This was the closest spot where we still felt like we were safe.

"Right now the fire is working through a thick stand of trees at a bend in the river about two miles from here. We don't think it's going to come this far east, but obviously we're keeping a careful eye on it. If it comes much closer, we'll have to push back east some more. And no one wants that."

He laughed to himself. "I think we'd all agree a hundred miles is long enough without having to double back."

"Yep," Cowgirl said.

"We've been on a hold for about"—he glanced at his watch—"ninety minutes now. I'm afraid all we can do is wait it out. The fire has been moving northeast pretty steadily, so we think it's going to move out eventually. But for now we're waiting it out."

"Got it."

"Once we think it's safe, we'll let you know. We're in touch with the Rangers and they've been using their spotting towers, so we've got a pretty good idea where the fire is. We're hoping it shouldn't be too long now. Then we'll give you your vet cards back, the clock will be restarted and you can get on your way.

"I know it's not ideal," Chambers finished. "But we've got to put safety first."

"I understand," Cowgirl said. "Thanks."

"Think we'll be released in time that we can get to Auburn and get our belt buckles?" Lizzy asked.

"I sure hope so, young lady," Chambers said. "But I'm afraid it's not up to me."

He pointed to the west, toward the orange glow. "It's up to that fire. And it doesn't really announce its intentions ahead of time."

Lizzy went off and found herself a comfortable bit of ground, away from where she might get accidentally stepped on by a horse, and collapsed. Whether the rest would actually do her any good was beside the point. It just felt heavenly not to be in the saddle.

Cowgirl walked over to a small group of riders who were standing around a lantern that had been placed on the ground. Duke Dawson was one of them.

"What do you say, Duke?" Cowgirl said, casually.

In the dim glow of the lantern, Cowgirl saw a few other riders cast a glance in her direction like they wished she hadn't asked.

"I'll tell you what I say, Juliet. This is just plain bull, that's what's I say," Duke said, likely not for the first time. "I overheard one of those radios squawking, and they said the fire is off the trail. It's been off the trail for twenty, thirty minutes now. We could have been through already, but they're holding us like a bunch of goddamn cows.

"I'm sure it's one of those insurance things. They think we're gonna sue if we over heat or something. It's the goddamn lawyers ruining the world, like usual. I told Hal Chambers I'd sign a waiver if he'd let me go but he wouldn't give me my damn card back. He's a banker. You ask me, bankers and lawyers are cut from the same cloth."

"So I've been sitting here for an hour-and-a-half now, just waitin'. And I'm getting stiff and cold. And Diesel's getting stiff and cold. And I got a cooler with some brews waiting for me at Auburn. I should have one of those in my right hand and the Tevis Cup in my left. Instead I'm waiting here, playing 'Mother May I' with a damn banker."

He stamped his foot impatiently, making one of his Clover Bar spurs jangle.

"Well, anyway," he said, suddenly recognizing his rant had made her uncomfortable. She had that look like she was going to try to slip away, and he wanted to keep talking with her. So he looked down, shoved his hands in his pockets, and came up with, "How's your ride been going?"

"Real good. Real good, thanks."

"You made it this far. That's something. Guess that mare isn't such a worthless piece after all."

"No, Duke. She's really a first-rate horse."

He waved her away. "I wasn't asking because I was fishing for a thank you. You deserve a good horse. You know I'd..."

His voice trailed off, then he came back with, "You know if you ever need anything from me, all you need to do is ask, right? I know those medical bills can be pretty steep. You still getting that help from the Cowboy Up Foundation? They giving you that check every month?"

Cowgirl couldn't keep the look of surprise off her face. "How do you know about that?"

"Oh, Betty's family and my family go way back," he said. "It's no big deal. Anyhow..."

Duke shook his head and cast an agitated glance toward where Hal Chambers was huddled with the three other volunteers who had stayed behind. Chambers had his ear to the radio.

"Hope they let us go soon," Duke continued. "Don't they know I got a cup to win? I was in first place when they put that hold on, you know. Had about a five-minute lead and everything. That damn cup was mine, and then the lawyers went and screwed up everything."

"Well, lawyers will tend to do that," a gentle voice said from behind them.

Cowgirl turned to see the tall form of Woolfolk Henry

limping toward her. "Wooly!" she said, brightly. "When did you get here?"

"Just now. How's your ride been?"

"Well, we're here," Cowgirl said, nodding toward Lizzy.

"So you are. Congratulations."

Wooly sidled up to Cowgirl and put his long arm around her, taking her in a half-hug for just a moment before he released it. Not many people even tried to touch Cowgirl. There was something in her demeanor that told them she simply wasn't open for hugs.

With Wooly, she didn't seem to mind so much.

Duke Dawson was glaring, so Cowgirl said, "Duke, this is Woolfolk Henry. Goes by Wooly."

Wooly held out his hand. "Howdy," he said.

"You a lawyer?" Duke replied.

"Yeah, why, you want to sue someone?" Wooly said, a playful grin on his face.

"Not feeling too friendly toward lawyers right now," Duke said, then walked away, leaving Wooly's outstretched hand behind.

"I sure charmed him," Wooly said, still amused. "What's the problem?"

"I wouldn't even know where to start," Cowgirl said. "How's your ride been?"

"Terrific. Laddy Boy has been incredible. There's just no quit in that horse this year. I really think he's going to make it this time. And it's all thanks to you and Lizzy, getting me over Cougar Rock. If we do get a buckle, Jack's name will join Laddy Boy's engraved on it."

Wooly was beaming at her. Then he coughed. "That's assuming this smoke doesn't take me out first."

"Yeah," Cowgirl said. "No kidding."

Just then a loud voice came calling from the middle of the clearing. It was Hal Chambers, "Your attention please. Can I get all the riders over here?"

He was soon surrounded by twenty-four people, all that remained from a group that had once numbered 199.

"Okay, thanks for your patience everyone," he said. "We have the word from the Rangers that the fire has jumped the river to the north. That's bad news for them, because it means it's heading for some homes over there. But it's good news for us, because it gives us a window to pass through.

"We need to stick together here. We've had fires on the trail before on other race days but for now, we can't have anyone separating from the group. It's just too dangerous out there and the Rangers are insisting we keep everyone accounted for. There's still a lot of fuel left on the south side of the river. If the fire doubles back, it could get ugly. So we're going to move out quickly and then stay in a single file line up through the affected area. Please be patient. We can only go as fast as our slowest horse. Once we get to the other side of No Hands Bridge, I'll give you your vet cards back and you'll be on your own from there. Any questions?"

No one spoke.

"Good," Chambers said. "Now we need someone to lead us. Obviously, it needs to be a steady horse with a nice, even temperament. A horse with good sense and good footing. A horse that won't spook. It's going to be a little scary out there, but if we have the right leader, I think we'll be okay."

It was Wooly who piped up and said, "Hal, we don't need a horse to lead us. What we need is a mule."

Chapter

25
Fire

WITHIN A VERY FEW MINUTES, twenty-four riders and four volunteers had saddled up with a minimum of conversation and fuss.

Wooly's nomination of Jack to lead the group had been accepted unopposed. Lizzy, who was thrilled to have her mule appointed to such an important task, gave him a quick pep talk.

It was one the mule didn't seem to need. There was a certain nobility to Jack as Lizzy led him around to the front of the group. His chin was a little higher than usual. His bearing was just a bit straighter.

He knew he had been both summoned and entrusted. Maybe not the exact specifics. But he knew.

Immediately behind Jack were Piper and Cowgirl, whose familiarity with the trail was better than most. And immediately behind them was Hal Chambers, whose familiarity was better than anyone's.

"Okay, everyone ready?" Chambers called out.

A chorus of yeses and okays—with one firm yep—followed.

"Anyone need us to wait?" Chambers asked.

No one answered.

"All right. Lead on, Jack."

Lizzy squeezed the mule's sides and off they went. They had agreed on a nice trot. It was four miles to No Hands Bridge, roughly a half-hour ride if all went well.

They passed the first mile without incident. It was just a line of riders, some with glow sticks and headlamps, some without. The air around them was growing even thicker to the point that now the full moon had been rendered indistinct. Its beams had been diffused by smoke, bouncing off in a thousand directions, creating a white haze in a dark night. Even the orange glow was now blotted out.

It was at the end of the second mile that they entered what had been, until so recently, the burn area. The landscape immediately turned black, like it was the nesting ground for Death itself.

Fires have been scouring the western forests of America for as long as there have been forests—and for far longer than there's been an America. For that reason, you'll always hear folks say forest fires are natural. But there is nothing very natural-looking about what they leave behind.

Charred spires of trees rose up from the ground, their limbs and needles scorched away. The brush had been obliterated, turned into great heaps of char. The devastation was so complete it seemed even the soil itself had burned.

Although there were no active flames remaining, there were still small hot spots where smoke rose, trailing away like hundreds of tiny chimneys. It made the riders feel like they were on a trip to Hades with the nearby American serving as their River Styx.

The horses had grown quiet. Only the sound of their hooves falling and their saddles squeaking could be heard.

The riders had gone mute, too. There was something about seeing the destructive power of that fire that brought a hush over them, plunging them into a kind of prayerful reverence.

The only thing breaking the silence was the squawking of Hal Chambers' radio.

"Whoa," he said. "Hold up, Lizzy. I need to listen to this."

Lizzy slowed Jack to a walk, then a stop. Every horse behind them did the same.

Chambers brought his radio up. "Hal here. Say again."

He frowned as the radio spit forth what sounded like little more than a burst of static. But he held it near his ear for another twenty seconds, listening intently.

When the transmission ended, he said, "Okay, roger that."

Even in the ghostly half-light, Cowgirl could see the consternation on his face.

"What's the matter?" she asked, riding closer to him.

"The fire has doubled back across the river," he said. "It's grown so big it's creating its own wind. And that wind is blowing south, the opposite direction it's been blowing this whole time."

He spoke softly enough that the other riders couldn't hear. He was mindful of the tough spot they were all in.

"So what does that mean, exactly?" Cowgirl asked.

"It means our escape route is cut off. It sounds like it's maybe a quarter mile behind us. The only way we can go now is forward."

"Well, that's not so bad, is it?"

"It is if the fire also doubles back ahead of us. We'd be trapped."

Chambers could not hide the fear on his face. A horse or a mule can outrun a forest fire as long as it has a trail to run on. If the trail was cut off, the animals would have to plunge into the brush—at which point their speed advantage would disappear.

"Well, I guess we better keep moving then," Cowgirl said.

"Yeah," Chambers said, getting his countenance back under control, then raising the volume of his voice back to a normal level. "Okay, Lizzy. Let's go."

Following orders, Lizzy continued leading them through the wasteland, passing the odd sight that was Pointed Rocks Ranch.

This was ordinarily the Tevis's last gate-and-go, a final check of the horses' health before they embark on the heroic end of their journey. The animals that make it that far tend to be supremely well conditioned, so it's really not much of an impediment for most teams. If anything, it's a jovial, giddy place, because the finish is so near.

Not on this night. It was abandoned, empty of the life it usually held, which made it seem somehow sinister. The veterinarians and other volunteers had been evacuated hours earlier. All of the tents had been taken down and hauled away when the trucks had been forced to flee.

The grasses that ordinarily covered the area had been burned down to the roots, leaving only black soot behind. A fine coating of ash covered the landscape, making it look eerie and otherworldly.

Lizzy kept Jack going at a good trot through the clearing, then plunged back into what had once been tall grass and scrub. The twenty-seven riders behind them followed dutifully for the next half mile as the fire damage slowly lessened.

It started with some of the larger, older trees. They had natural defenses against fires and had therefore survived; even if the smaller trees and underbrush near them had all burned. Before long, they entered an area where the middling trees were also unscathed. Then, very quickly, they crossed the line and were back into forest completely untouched by fire, having been spared by winds that had pushed the flames in the other direction.

Just as it had been strange to be in a landscape that was

completely black, it was nearly as strange to again be back in one that was all green.

The smell of the fire was every bit as strong and acrid as it had been, but the smoke was nearly gone. The wind had definitely shifted to the south, and it was now carrying the smoke away with it.

It literally cleared the air. Which meant that when they crested a small ridge, they had a perfect view of what was greeting them in the valley below. A wall of fire, heading their way.

It was as if the sky had gone ablaze. Huge flame tongues licked the night from the tops of the trees. Their trunks glowed orange, red and yellow.

Lizzy was the first to see it. She let out a yelp that neither Cowgirl, nor Hal Chambers, nor any of the riders needed help translating as soon as they saw what prompted it.

It was an understandable instinct to pull back on the reins, not wanting to send herself or her mule any closer. But as soon as Lizzy began slowing Jack to a walk, Cowgirl's authoritative voice boomed out.

"Keep going," she said. "You have to keep going."

"But Mom—"

"We can't go back. The fire is closing in behind us, too."

"But—"

"You have to go, now!" Cowgirl said. "The trail bends to the left about a half mile from here. If we can make it there before the fire, we'll be able to outrun it. It's our only chance. Go now. Fast as you can."

Lizzy was frozen for a moment. Cowgirl quickly rode up behind her and said, "*Yee-ha!*"

At the same moment, Lizzy came out of her trance and squeezed her heels into Jack's sides. The mule sprang forward. Piper and Cowgirl were close behind, followed by

Hal Chambers and the rest of the group.

To anyone who didn't know what was happening, it would have looked like suicide: a line of riders, rushing toward an inferno just as fast as their mounts could go. But, at the moment, it was the best of several very bad options.

Fact was, if they stood where they were, they'd be in trouble even sooner. Fire goes uphill faster than it does down. And there was no question the top of the ridge would soon be incinerated—if not from behind them, then certainly from ahead. The flames were spreading rapidly across the valley below them as the wind, generated by the enormous power of the fire behind it, pushed the front edge forward.

Lizzy could feel the heat on her face as surely as she could the fear in her stomach. Jack was galloping, as was every horse behind him, and they were covering huge chunks of ground. There was just no telling whether his top speed would be good enough.

For the next half mile, the geometry was working cruelly against them. They were riding west. The fire was spreading south, perpendicular to them. For as fast they were going, they weren't gaining on it.

Quite the opposite. It was gaining on them.

As Lizzy descended into the valley, heading toward the bend in the trail that might offer salvation, the fire was spitting out embers that were landing on all sides of them. Some landed harmlessly. Others found dry piles of pine needles that instantly ignited.

Lizzy passed a twenty-foot-tall stand of manzanita that was already ablaze. It was quickly igniting the trees around it.

The wind gusted, pushing a hail of embers on the trail. One landed on Lizzy's leg, leaving a black mark on her chaps.

Soot and ash were floating everywhere now. The fire was literally booming so loud it drowned out the rushing of the nearby river.

Lizzy coughed. Her eyes watered. The smoke was getting thick again. The bandana across her face could only filter so much. It was like the world was suddenly running out of oxygen.

"Go, Jack," she yelled, as she felt the mule's speed beginning to drop. "Keep going, boy."

She squeezed his sides harder. They raced past a tall ponderosa whose higher branches had ignited. The fire was closing over top of them. From behind, one of the horses—Piper perhaps, or maybe Hal Chambers' mount—let out a terrified whinny.

They weren't going to make it. That was what the horse seemed to be saying. And it was certainly the thought going through Lizzy's head. The fire seemed to be everywhere now.

Another chunk of underbrush, this one right next to the trail, was burning brightly. The heat radiating away from it was incredible. It seared through her T-shirt and pressed against her face.

She kept riding. She had no choice. A pile of pine straw at the base of a tree was ablaze and the flames were now licking up the trunk.

Lizzy became aware the sweat was pouring off of her, thicker than it had during the worst of the canyons. There was just heat and fire and more heat. All over. Everywhere.

She wondered what it would feel like to be burned alive. Would she pass out from all the smoke first? Or would it be an unspeakable agony as her flesh blistered and sizzled?

The heat was so intense she had to close her eyes. It hurt too much to keep them open. She leaned forward and clung to Jack's neck.

The big mule powered ahead, almost oblivious to the inferno that was closing in on all sides. He seemed to know he carried the fate of not only his own beloved rider, but also of every team behind him. Horses will follow a leader. The line needed that leader to be strong. And there was no animal in that flaming forest as strong—in body or in will—as Jack.

One steady stride at a time, Jack kept chewing up ground, his hooves pounding as the flames shot around him. The oven door was closing on them, but Jack was determined to keep going as long as there was even a sliver of an opportunity for escape.

Lizzy's face was tingling. The sweat was evaporating almost as soon as it sprang onto her brow. She wondered if her eyebrows would burst into flame like a pine straw pile.

And then Lizzy felt the most incredible thing: a slight pull on the right side of her body, on the right rein. Jack was turning left. She dared to open her eyes. They had made it to the bend. There were still flames on all sides, but as she looked down the trail, there was definitely less of them in the direction they were now heading.

They were finally running away from the fire. They were making their way toward the green and away from the orange and yellow and black.

"Good boy, Jack," she yelled. "Good boy!"

The heat slowly dropped. As they entered an area where nothing was ablaze, she stood in her stirrups. The euphoria—she was going to live, they were *all* going to live—had overtaken her. She let out a loud, clear, "Yeeee ha!" Then she hoisted her splinted hand, high in the air.

Just like a real rodeo cowboy. Just like her dad used to do when he was the best bull rider in America.

Chapter

26
"Go"

THEY WERE WELL BEYOND Pointed Rocks Ranch, putting more distance between themselves and the advancing fire.

Then it was on to No Hands Bridge. The span, which towers more than two hundred feet over the American river, was built for the railroad in the early 20th Century, then abandoned mid-way through it. Runners, hikers and horses started using it to cross the river, even though it had no railing. During an early running of the Tevis, a fine and fearless horsewoman dropped her reins as she crossed and boasted, "Look, Ma. No hands!"

With those words, a piece of Tevis lore was born; and a formerly anonymous railroad bridge got a new name.

There was no such jubilance among these twenty-four riders. The exhilaration of outrunning the fire proved to be short-lived. As they trudged across the bridge in a single-file line, they were quiet. The adrenaline had worn off, to be replaced by a fatigue that was both physical and mental. The reality of how close they had come to catastrophe had a sobering, exhausting effect.

Once they were safely on the other side—now separated from the fire by a rushing band of water—the riders dismounted, congregated and took stock of injuries.

One rider's hair was singed. An asthmatic was using his inhaler. One of the horses had a burn on his flank. Another was lame, having shied, veered off the trail, and taken an awkward step.

But, on the whole, the injuries were not serious compared to what might have been. They were alive and thankful to be so.

Hal Chambers was soon walking over to the group that had gathered. "Okay," he said. "I've radioed the Forest Rangers and told them we made it through. It sounds like we were pretty lucky. The whole south side of the river is on fire right now."

He let that sink in for a moment. No one needed to be told how close they had come to eternity.

"As you recall from your pre-ride instructions, the Southern Pacific Railroad has agreed to stop the trains for the evening, so we won't have the race finish short of the tracks like we usually do. We're going to finish at McCann Stadium this year. You'll enter the stadium from the side, then do a half lap around the track to the finish line. Got it?"

No one replied, so he held a stack of well-worn cards in the air. "I've got your vet cards here. When I call your name, please come take your card. You'll have to present them to the vets after you finish, of course."

Chambers read off the names. One by one, the twenty-four survivors walked up and claimed their cards. When the final card was disbursed, Chambers spoke for the last time.

"Okay. It's now"—he looked down at his watch—"One o'clock in the morning, on the dot. The hold is over. I'm going to radio ahead and tell them to restart the official clock. You're all free to go."

The riders were about to disperse, but a loud voice interrupted them, "Wait a second, aren't we going to do a restart?"

It was Duke Dawson. He had taken the center of attention that Chambers had just vacated.

"That's up to you all," Chambers said.

"Well, then, come on now. You're in charge. Take charge. Let's go," Dawson said taking over. "There's still a cup at stake here. We got three miles to the finish and some horse and rider are gonna win this thing. Let's line up and have ourselves a good, honest horserace. I bet that stadium in Auburn is full of people right now. Let's give 'em a good show."

The other riders exchanged glances. None of them were in the mood for a race or a show. Not after what they had been through.

"Let's just ride to Auburn together," a voice in the darkness suggested. "We'll enter the stadium together and cross the finish line at the same time."

"What? And have a tie?" Duke asked, sounding incredulous.

"Yeah, a twenty-four-way tie for the Tevis Cup. It seems only right. We'll let the mule lead us."

Most of the riders were nodding. A few voiced agreement.

"Now, that's the damndest thing I've ever heard," Duke said. "There's a spot right over here that's wide enough for all of us. We can line up, someone can say 'Go,' and we can be off. Right, Hal? That way the best horse and rider win the Tevis Cup, just like it's supposed to be."

The proclamation was met with silence.

"Aww, come on now. You can't be serious. You really want to follow a mule all the way to Auburn"?

"Yeah, as a matter of fact, we do," said another voice. "That mule saved us."

"Goddamn," Duke spat. "You've come ninety-seven miles through lightning, flood, and fire and you want to walk to the finish behind a mule...like a goddamn mule rain?"

He looked over toward Cowgirl. "Come on, Juliet. Two houses, 'both alike in dignity,' having themselves a horserace. What do you say? I know you want to win that big shiny cup just as much as I do."

Cowgirl was shaking her head. "Yes, I do. And if Jack leads us, we can *all* win."

Duke shook his head. "I can't believe you all. Geez."

He stormed over to Diesel and swung up on the stallion. Duke touched his spurs to the horse's side and, despite its apparent agitation, brought him over to where the group was still assembled, the horse straining at the bit the whole way.

"I'm gonna go now," he threatened. "Come on. A couple of you have to want to go with me. Let's do this right."

No one said anything.

"I won't feel bad about winning. I was in the lead when they stopped this thing. I should have won by now. Come on, someone give me an honest race."

There was, again, silence.

"Well, be that way. Okay. One of you shout 'Go.' Shout the start for me and my stallion here so we can go win us the cup."

The stallion reared a little in response to Duke's very tight rein. Twenty-three pairs of lips remained absolutely still.

"Come on," Duke said. "Give the call. Someone say 'Go' for us."

Silence prevailed.

And then, from the darkness, came a firm voice.

"Just go," it said.

It was Cowgirl's.

Duke Dawson did not need to be told twice. He dug his spurs into Diesel's sides and raced off.

Twenty-two riders watched him disappear into the night, then turned toward their own mounts, readying themselves to swing into their saddles and walk the final three miles.

One did not. He made a straight line toward Cowgirl.

"Why don't you go?" Wooly asked her.

Cowgirl looked up toward Wooly.

"Because Piper likes to stay with Jack," she said. "And these riders need Jack to lead them."

"Well, Cowgirl, actually not. We're good. We needed Jack during the fire, but not anymore. We can all make it the fairground stadium just fine without him."

"You help other riders," Cowgirl said. "That's the way the Tevis works."

"Cowgirl," Wooly said tenderly. "You hauled me up over Cougar Rock. You saved Clemmy at El Dorado Canyon. You've done your share of helping others today. Go on. Go win the Tevis."

"Thanks, Wooly," she said, pausing. "You're kind. But—"

"I never tell war stories," he said hesitantly, in a voice that was suddenly quite different and more serious than any Cowgirl had ever heard before.

"There's nothing worse than a shot-up Vietnam veteran who won't shut up about a war no one cares about anymore. But a few days after I was hit"—he pointed down to his legs—"a young second lieutenant was appointed as my relief."

"A week after that, the young lieutenant was killed by a sniper. It was then, I promised myself to capture every opportunity life gave me. That's why I ride the Tevis. Not because I'm much of a horseman, and not because my legs are really up to the ride."

"Now," he said. "This is your opportunity—a gift you may never get again. You owe it to yourself and your husband to take it. Because maybe *you* don't care about who wins. But who do you think Cowboy would rather see cross the finish line first? You or Duke Dawson?"

Lizzy was already up on Jack.

"Come on, Mom. Let's go. You know this is Daddy's

dream."

Cowgirl cast her glance between Wooly and her daughter, now ganging up on her.

"Mom, you're wasting time," Lizzy said.

Cowgirl had shoved her hands in her front pockets.

"If you don't go right now, I'm going without you," Lizzy threatened. "And you know Jack and Piper won't like that."

"Right," Cowgirl said. Out came her hands as she took ten long strides to where Piper was standing and vaulted into the saddle.

"Woo hoo!" Lizzy shouted.

Wooly smiled, "Go get him, you two!"

"Tevis riders, the last part of the trail is now open," Wooly announced.

"Go!"

Chapter

27

Black Hole of Calcutta

PIPER AND JACK TORE OFF, the Arab first, the mule second, just like it had been on so many starlit training rides around Lodi.

The Western States Trail coming away from No Hands Bridge is an abandoned railroad grade. It's smooth and fast, the closest the Tevis comes to a groomed racetrack. It's easy to make good time on it.

It then ducks onto a single track trail through the forest, where the going is slower. Then it bursts out on the railroad grade again. Then back into the forest.

For Cowgirl and Lizzy, it was like some kind of carnival ride, one that veers in and out and up and down, always throwing some kind of surprise: a branch here, a rock there, a dip or a rise in the trail that doesn't become apparent until it's already happened.

They were flying through the night, more feeling than seeing. They were both standing in their stirrups. The wind rushed past their faces. Their blond braids—one for the mother, two for the daughter—bounced against their backs.

It was when the trail veered back onto the railroad grade for the third time that they finally caught sight of Duke Dawson. He had been poking along at a gentle pace, unaware that the horserace he so badly wanted was coming up behind him.

In the full moonlight, Cowgirl could see him cast a backward glance. He had certainly heard them. When he saw them, a smile flashed across his face. Then he turned his attention forward. He buried his spurs in Diesel's sides again. Cowgirl was perhaps a hundred yards behind now. But even with Diesel springing back to life, she was gaining. There was no question Piper was the better horse. For all her nerves and occasional tantrums, there was no finer equine athlete at the Tevis that year. And Cowgirl had ridden her efficiently, especially in the early going. All that "wisely and slow" was now paying off. Even after ninety-seven miles, Piper had speed to burn left in her legs.

Jack did not. But he was stubborn. And sometimes, stubborn is just as good as fast.

So is loyalty. For Jack, now busting a lung to keep up, it wasn't as much about reeling in Duke Dawson as it was about keeping pace with Piper. He knew how much his friend needed his comforting presence.

The only question, really, was whether there was enough distance left for them to catch up. They were already a mile into the three miles that remained. And a hundred yards is a fairly significant head start in a two-mile race.

Piper charged on all the same. It's a good thing horses have never been very good at math, because she didn't know how lousy her odds were. Her legs were beating the fastest cadence of her life.

Jack was flattening himself out, almost like he was streamlining his big body. He was mere strides behind.

The final time the trail leaves the railroad grade, it plunges onto a section formally known as the Trail to Calcutta Falls. But Tevis riders have another name for it: The Black Hole of Calcutta.

They call it that because even the fastest riders reach it

long after the sun has set. And while the Tevis is contested during the full moon, it doesn't matter in the Black Hole of Calcutta. The trail at that point is overhung with fig trees, whose hugely broad leaves overlap in such a way that they block out all light from above—whether it's sunlight or moonlight.

Even during the daytime, it leaves the trail in a kind of permanent dusk. At night, it becomes jet black. Cowgirl and Lizzy literally couldn't see their hands in front of their faces.

They rode on all the same, trusting in Piper and Jack. They couldn't see Duke Dawson anymore, but they could hear him somewhere up ahead, swearing at his sweating horse, exhorting Diesel to find an extra gear he simply didn't have.

They were definitely making up ground. How much and how fast, they couldn't tell.

Soon, they came on a creek. For a brief moment, the fig trees parted. They could see Duke Dawson up ahead, but only seventy-five yards now.

Piper barely slowed as she splashed over, her hooves seeming to skim across the surface of the water. Lizzy felt the drops hitting her face moments later.

Then it was back into the black hole. Cowgirl bent forward, trying to make herself low so she'd be less of a target for the vegetation that seemed to be springing out of nowhere, whacking her face.

Somewhere up ahead the sound of Diesel's hoof strikes were getting closer. Duke Dawson was banging his spurred heels into the horse's ribs, trying to cajole more speed out of the stallion.

Piper didn't need to be urged on. The mare was already redoubling her efforts. Ask any jockey: the best horses, the ones that become champions, simply have a will to win. And this was the first time Cowgirl was realizing just how immense Piper's will was.

Another mile had passed. There was just one more to go now. They emerged from the fig grove and galloped on toward Robie Point, a half mile away. The moonlight was illuminating their labors once again. They could see Duke Dawson, now just forty yards ahead.

The trail entered a series of uphill switchbacks that forced him to slow. Yet for Cowgirl, this almost made it like the barrel racing she had done in her past life as a rodeo champion. She leaned into the turns, allowing Piper to pick up another few feet with each bend.

By the time they made it to the wide, dirt fire road that led to the fairgrounds and McCann Stadium, Dawson's lead had been shaved to ten yards. There was less than a half mile to go. A hundred-mile race had come down to the last two thousand feet.

The road turned to the right. Diesel was taking up the middle of the path, so Cowgirl eased toward the inside.

Piper bore down, perfectly in sync with what her rider wanted her to do. She was taking in streams of air and snorting them back out as her nostrils flared. Her hooves, so finely shod by Choppy, were digging into the soft ground, bringing it up in small clods as she fairly flew across it.

Jack, incredibly, was still right on her tail, giving this final charge every last ounce of his considerable strength.

Duke Dawson kept glancing back. The lead was now eight yards. Then six. Whether Piper could see her former owner or smell him, I don't know. But it was like the idea had now been firmly implanted in her twenty-ounce brain: that if she could find a little more speed, she could break the heart of the man who had once been so compelled to break her spirit.

She poured it on, somehow accelerating even when it seemed like she couldn't possibly go any faster. Her muscles strained and the sweat poured off her and she gained a yard, then another.

Duke didn't need to look back any more. The mare was now in his peripheral vision. He buried his spurs into Diesel's sides repeatedly, digging at the horse's hide until tiny red flecks started showing. He yelled and swore. He spurred some more, with all the strength his legs could muster and all the force his boots could bring. It didn't matter. Diesel had been berated, cursed, and spiked for ninety-nine and a half miles. The horse simply didn't have anything left.

The moment Piper drew even with him, Diesel flat out gave up, quitting as stallions are sometimes famous for doing. He slowed from a gallop to a trot to a walk and then he just stopped. No measure of Duke Dawson's cruelty could make the horse so much as move.

Piper sailed past, striding smoothly and beautifully, like she was in a pasture by herself, running for sheer joy.

Cowgirl didn't say a word as she flashed by. Her silence said it all. But she couldn't stop the swell of pride she felt in her horse, nor could she staunch the thought that filled her head as she and Piper left Duke Dawson in their dust: Not bad for a worthless piece of shit.

Chapter

28

Finish Line

THE STADIUM WAS IN SIGHT, its huge lights bathing the crowd below in a soft glow made hazy from all the smoke in the air.

On the top step of the bleachers, a few of the spectators had turned around so they could keep an eye on the trail. Many of them had started the day as competitors, so they watched that final horserace drama play out with their breath held.

As soon as Piper made her final move, one of the spectators high up turned around and announced in a loud voice, "It's Cowgirl! Cowgirl's gonna win! And her daughter is right behind her. They're gonna win the Tevis!"

The words floated down to the side of the quarter mile oval track, where Doc, Choppy, Miss Betty were standing and Cowboy was sitting, maybe a hundred feet beyond the finish line.

Doc was speechless. His big arms fell to the side. The last time he had seen Cowgirl and Lizzy they were in 47th and 48th place, respectively. This was beyond anything he had considered possible.

Choppy started jumping up and down. His lips were

spread into a smile that covered half his face, his gold tooth glinting under the stadium lights. He was banging Doc on the back.

"*Dios mio! Dios mio! Virgin de Guadalupe, gracias! Gracias!*" he howled. "Can you believe it? Can you believe it?"

Miss Betty brought her hands to her mouth, like she had just been given the perfect gift on Christmas morning. There were already tears welling in the tough old woman's eyes, enough that she was momentarily speechless.

Cowboy sat there, his head lolled to one side, his face perfectly vacant.

The crowd was perhaps too stunned to respond at first—the *mother-daughter* team winning the Tevis? But now people were standing. A cheer was coming up ragged at first, but growing. Many of the people offering the cheer had been awake since dawn the day before, but that only seemed to stoke their enthusiasm.

Cowgirl could hear the noise swelling in the distance as she aimed Piper toward the side entrance. By the time she burst into the stadium, it was at a full and exuberant roar.

Piper responded to the moment in exactly the way you'd expect, holding her head high, perking up her tail. Any hint that she was worn out from what had essentially been a three-mile sprint could not be detected in her prideful strides.

Jack, a length or two behind her, as always, just churned his legs, ever the quiet warrior. Lizzy smiled through the now-persistent throbbing in her legs, sitting as straight and tall as she could in her saddle.

They had only half a track-length remaining. Two turns to go. It was a moment Cowgirl had thought about many times, during cold winter nights or on long training rides. She had long imagined having only one-eighth of a mile left in the Tevis, with nothing of consequence between her and the belt buckle she coveted.

She had just never considered the moment would play out like this. Whenever she had finished the Tevis before, it was always after five o'clock in the morning, more than twenty-four hours after she had started, when the stadium had all but emptied out, when the satisfaction of completion was hers alone.

Now, here she was with hundreds of people to share her joy. She had Piper going at a nice lope. Not a neck-breaking pace like before, but still a good clip.

Soon she was into the final turn. The crowd was really making a racket now. So many of the Tevis people knew her. They knew what had happened to Cowboy. They knew how much she had struggled. They knew about her repeated failures and, more importantly, her refusal to accept them.

This is the kind of stuff Tevis folks are made of. The mountains and canyons make the race a spectacle, but it's the people who make it special. She was surely one of them. And so they were thrilled for her victory, now just mere seconds away.

Cowgirl was closing in on the finish line. Just thirty feet to go. Then twenty. She was sitting in her saddle, a serene look on her face, a horsewoman in total control at the end of a historic and historically difficult ride.

And then suddenly her right foot was out of the stirrup. Her right leg was swinging up and back. Her upper body leaned toward Piper's neck for just a moment as her hips cleared away from the saddle. Her right leg had now joined her left leg on Piper's left side. Then her left foot pulled out of the stirrup. Her strong arms pushed away from Piper's neck and she let go of the reins.

She was airborne for an instant. And then she jumped off. Her red pointy-toed boots landed easily on the soft dirt.

Cowgirl had jumped off five feet short of the finish line.

She had done it so quickly Lizzy couldn't have reacted if she wanted to. She didn't even sense what was happening until it was too late. She and her mule had already crossed the finish line.

The Tevis had never been won by a mule of any sex, color or age.

But in 1985 it was won by a gelded, bay, eight-year-old mule.

His name was Jack.

Lizzy brought Jack to a halt just beyond the line, gave the mule a quick pat then jogged toward her mother, not knowing if she was happy, grateful, or distressed. She was definitely confused.

"Mom, why did you do that?" Lizzy said. "You were about to win the Tevis! It was Daddy's dream!"

"Oh, baby," Cowgirl said, cupping her daughter's face. "*This* was your father's dream. He was always quite clear: Lizzy will finish first. It was always Lizzy will finish first."

Lizzy bit her lip. And then she turned and headed for her dad, for Cowboy.

Or, I guess I should just say it straight up...

For me.

It had been eight years since my body had responded to a single command I gave it. Eight years is nearly three thousand days, some huge number of hours. And I can tell you that in all that time, I had never been so desperate for it to finally listen to me.

I wanted nothing more in the universe than to reach my arms out for my brave, beautiful, loving daughter and hug her properly, like a father should. I wanted my throat to make the sounds that would tell her how proud of her I was. I wanted to smother her face with tiny kisses like I did when she was a little girl.

And so I screwed up every bit of determination I could summon, every ounce of gumption I ever used to hang onto a bucking Brahman, every IOU I had been banking against my Maker for eight years now—those "if you will...then I promise to..." type things.

Back in the days when I could walk and ride and recite poetry, they always did say: there goes a cowboy who's full of try.

And I tried. Oh, man, did I try. Lizzy was closing in on me, beaming that special smile of hers, and I'd like to be able to tell you I reached out for her; that I somehow pulled off the miracle that would have been pulling my wrecked body out of that chair. That I lifted my girl high in the sky and then gave her a hug that she'd remember forever.

Alas, no. All I did was sit there in my chair, trapped in my motionless body.

Lizzy hugged me and kissed me all the same. God bless that dear child. I prayed she knew how much her daddy loved her, even if he didn't have a way in the world of showing it.

"We did it, Daddy. We did it!" she squealed. "I won the Tevis, just like you always said I would."

Cowgirl—my Cowgirl—came next. She bent down toward me and kissed my cheek, her lips soft like rose petals, like they always were.

And, yes, I could feel it. I can't explain the science behind it, but even though I couldn't make my body work worth a damn, I could see and hear and feel everything that happened to me over those thousands of days. Oh, man, could I feel.

That feeling—my wife touching me—that was the best thing. It was what had made my miserable life worth living for eight years now, truth be told. Her touches. One at a time.

And, thank God, she somehow knew how much they sustained me. Because she kept blessing me with them.

I will tell you, if love could restore motion to a crippled

man's legs, I would have leapt out of my chair and danced; and if love could restore sound to a mute man's voice, I would have lifted my chin in song; and if love could allow an expressionless man to show emotion, I would have smiled a smile like you've never seen in your entire life.

Because their love was that strong. It was stronger than a lightning strike. Stronger than a forest fire. Stronger than Jack's will to continue. Stronger than Piper's will to win.

And I'm sure a lot of people looked at me during that final day—or in any of the three thousand days that preceded it, really—and said, wow, what a tough break that poor son of a gun had.

I didn't.

All I could think about was how lucky I had been for the women who loved me to the end and beyond.

Epilogue

LATER, AFTER THE PRESENTATION of the Tevis Cup, they rolled me off to a nearby motel that Doc had arranged for us. Lizzy sat silently next to me in the cozy room. There, they told stories until well after the sun rose.

That's where I heard more about how they climbed the mountains, traversed the canyons, and crossed the rivers and streams. I heard about Last Chance and the mosquitoes. About Pucker Point. About quiet Jack getting it in his big mule head to bellow out that series of hee-haws. About Choppy spiking those ranch hands' beers.

I also heard how Duke Dawson asked Cowgirl about the Cowboy Up Foundation. Cowgirl had a little frown on her face as she talked about that with Miss Betty.

"It's not a big deal, really," Cowgirl said. "But did you... did you tell Duke Dawson about the money from the Cowboy Up Foundation?"

And this, of course, caused Miss Betty to purse her lips and knit her brow.

"Oh, child," she said, at last. "It's about time you know about the Cowboy Up Foundation."

"What do you mean?"

Miss Betty sighed. "Girl, Duke Dawson *is* the Cowboy

Up Foundation. Those monthly fist fulls have been coming from him."

Cowgirl just stood there. I have to say I was a little shocked myself.

"That's Duke for you," she continued. "I've known him since he was baby. And I know he's a lot to take sometimes. But that boy—man, I should say—well, he has good in his heart. Somewhere. Deep down under all that bluster.

"So after our friend here had his wreck, well, Duke knew you were in a bad way. But he also knew you wouldn't accept help. Especially his help. And he knew I was just kind of wasting away. And so he came up to me one day and said, 'Miss Betty, wanna do something really wonderful?' And he cooked up this plan where I was to come to your door, like a stray off the street, to help you out. And, I was going to tell you about the Cowboy Up Foundation."

"Anyhow," she said, letting out a big gust of breath in one big woof, "Every month for these last years, that check from the Cowboy Up Foundation has really been coming from Mr. Duke Dawson. And there you go."

"I...I..." Cowgirl stammered, unusually rendered at a loss for words.

"That man does love you," Miss Betty said.

Cowgirl looked down at her boots.

"I know, child. I know. Can't tell a heart where to point."

Cowgirl said nothing.

It was too soon for her. But not for me. And among my prayers was that Cowgirl's heart would someday know where to point again.

Sometime after that, there was a knock at the hotel room door.

It was Hal Chambers.

He was exhausted having been up for more than twenty-four hours. But he was still looking all straight and proper, like he had news to deliver.

"I hope I'm not interrupting,," he said, apologetically.

"Naw, come on in," Miss Betty said. "We were just telling lies."

He smiled.

"Well," he said. "The Western States Trail Foundation Veterinarians Committee has met and it has awarded the Haggin Cup to Piper."

He held a shiny trophy out toward Cowgirl, who bowed slightly as she accepted it, whether she meant to or not.

"Well, this is unexpected," she said.

"And why is that?"

"Well, because of the marks Vernon Puce put down on my vet card. He dinged me pretty good. That and I...I mean, we didn't even finish, technically. I jumped off. I didn't think I'd even be eligible for a buckle."

Hal Chambers was quiet for a moment. Then he got this funny little half-grin on his face.

"Well" he said. "Sure, that could be one way to look at it.

"There was something of a spirited debate over just those subjects. The Colonel, of all people, was arguing in your favor. I've never seen him so passionate. And Dr. Puce was arguing against it. He was pretty heated too. The person who broke the deadlock was Clementine."

"Clemmy?"

"Clementine Hearthstone. The woman with heat stroke you and Piper helped. You know she's the Board Chair of the Western States Trail Foundation, right?"

Cowgirl actually blushed a little. "Didn't know that, how's she doing?"

"Well, she is. And she's doing just fine, thanks to you. The first thing she did once the hospital released her was find the Vet Committee. She built the case that any horse that hauled eighty pounds of ice to save the life of another rider was more deserving of the Haggin Cup than any horse she was aware of. And she made a finer point that because you and Piper added two miles to your journey with your ice run, you really *did* complete the full hundred miles together, which is what the Tevis is all about. So not only should you win a buckle, you ought to be fully eligible for the Haggin. And the rest of the Vet Committee agreed with her. So Vernon was easily overruled."

Cowgirl looked at the trophy which seemed almost too big for the small motel room where we were crowded. Cowgirl bit her upper lip in hesitation.

"Piper and I thank you," she said at last.

"You're welcome, indeed," Chambers said. "You had a fine ride. A ride like I've never seen, that's for sure. Well... Clementine is not the only one in your debt."

Chambers looked down at his feet, then brought his gaze back up before speaking. "Cowgirl, I really doubted you. We all doubted you. Yesterday morning, if you had asked me, I would have told you it would take miracle for one of you to win, much less one of you to win it on a mule.

"You made believers out of all of us. And isn't the world a better place when you can believe in miracles?"

"Suppose it is," Cowgirl said. Now she was the one with her head down.

Chambers just nodded, then announced his departure. As soon as the door closed behind him, Cowgirl turned to the big veterinarian.

"Doc," she said. "This Haggin Cup is yours."

He started to protest.

"As Miss Betty would say, 'you hush child,'" Cowgirl interrupted him. "No way Piper and Jack would have been ready to run this race without you."

"Well," Doc said, with a big lump in his throat. "Thanks, Cowgirl. Thanks."

Cowgirl smiled. I think I had tears leaking out of my eyes

at that point. But, of course, it wasn't because of anything she said. It was because I didn't have control over it.

Nor could I control what happened next. I could feel it, of course. Because I could feel everything. And this is what I felt.

My eyes slowly losing focus. My whole body failing. The end I had been hoping to forestall approaching. My turn to cross the finish line coming near.

I had always thought that the world would just suddenly go black on me. The truth was a little more subtle than that as the truth often is. Things sort of faded gently. There was definitely a gray before the black. And it allowed my one good final look at my daughter and my wife. My blondies.

The last thought I had—and thank God for it—was that they were going to be okay without me. Yes, Cowgirl would be mourning for a while. But she had a lot of life left to live. And it was going to be a good and happy life, no matter what objections she had to the whole concept of happiness. She had too much spirit to be kept down.

And Lizzy? I might not have known it until those final twenty-four hours of my life, but I knew she was going to be fine, too. She was going to find a new dream, without her violin. But I was now certain she would keep going until she found it. And then she would work very hard to capture it.

She had too much of her mother in her—and maybe just the right amount of her father—to possibly be stopped.

At that point, it was time. I took in a slow breath, then let it go, content in knowing my last story had finally been told.

CPSIA information can be obtained
at www.ICGtesting.com
Printed in the USA
LVHW082225280820
664462LV00005B/90

9 781732 813717